Dedication

To my beloved wife, Brenda, and my three wonderful children, Deana, Danika, and Dallas, who patiently endured the writing of this book without quitting on me.

Acknowledgments

A special thanks to Steve and Miriam Simmons for all their hard work in the transcribing and editing of this text.

Endorsements

The principles enunciated in his book, *The Quitting Point*, have been aptly demonstrated in the life of its author, Michael Amico. The two words most easily said by one are, "I quit!" When faced in life with making ultimate choices in a heart-wrenching time, Mike, under God, decided to persevere. He writes from this premise. The noble purpose of this book, which is so well written, is to provide both vehicle and incentive, the inner God-given compulsion, to cross the finish line with faith, grace, and success. This text offers inspiration in your running to win.

Almon M. Bartholomew
Northeast Area Executive Presbyter
of the Assemblies of God

Mike Amico's message is one of hope and inspiration as he shares his powerful testimony in the book, *The Quitting Point*. God has used his dynamic preaching ministry to touch thousands with a challenge of revival and restoration. I am sure that his book will also encourage the reader to put his or her faith in God, even in the most desperate situation.

Lillian E. Sparks
Assemblies of God Women's Ministries Director
Pennsylvania-Delaware District

"I can identify with that." I don't know how many times that thought came to mind as I read through Michael's book, *The Quitting Point*. It is full of practical and vivid illustrations from everyday life that encourage us to not only face, but also press through, the difficult places. I highly recommend the author and his book.

Steve Brown
District Superintendent
South Carolina Assemblies of God

Michael Amico's book, *The Quitting Point*, offers inspiration based on the eternal truths of God's Word to those going through difficult times. I recommend this book to anyone who needs to press through the barriers of "Heartbreak Hill." Michael gives his readers a winning formula for persevering.

Dr. David G. Watson
Pastor
Central Assembly of God, Springfield, MO

Contents

Introduction

There is absolutely nothing easy about living in a pressure-cooker age. Every day we face the constant pressure of duties, deadlines, and demands. And no one is exempt: To put it in golfer's lingo, pressure is just "par for the course."

Most of us don't handle pressure well. When the pressure's on, most of us choose flight over fight and quit over stick. My purpose in writing this book is to prevent as many tragedies as possible, ranging from the simple resignation of responsibility to divorce and suicide.

Every day our fuses burn. Tempers flare, nerves snap, hearts break, and people quit. Welcome to the real world! Heart attacks, hypertension, nervous breakdowns, ulcers, and depression are just symptoms of a very dangerous disorder called stress. It's no surprise that two thirds of all doctor's office visits are prompted by stress-related symptoms.

You might appear to have it all together, but we know that sometimes what you see isn't what you get. If you're part of that 1 percent of society that really does have it all together, this book might not be for you; but if you're like the other struggling 99 percent of us, you'll want to read on. Beneath the surface, you might feel as if you're slowly coming apart at the seams. There may be a time bomb ticking away. The fuse has been lit, and you're about to explode.

If you feel like you are enrolled in the "school of hard knocks" and your "major" is *pressure*, I want to introduce you to a friend named *perseverance*. If you ever hope to stand firm and pass your course—apart from quitting—you'll need to get to know this friend. Perseverance is your only safeguard when the pressure's on and quitting seems the thing to do. When it comes to handling stress, perseverance is the master.

While writing this book, perseverance and I have become more deeply acquainted—in fact, I have learned more about the subject than through all my years of training and marathon running combined. Juggling a family, a full-time ministry, and a hectic traveling schedule is no piece of cake. Throw in an extra project, and you've got a pressure cooker. At times, I wanted to quit. But I've also discovered that it's only at the pressure points of life that we really learn how to persevere.

Because we often forget how to persevere, God is faithful to throw in a refresher course from time to time. Study hard and learn well, my fellow student, for the fight is tense and the race is long.

1

The Quitting Point

Our greatest glory consists not in never falling, but in rising every time we fall.

—Ralph Waldo Emerson

"Quit! Give up! You're beaten! You can't succeed!" The voices sound and resound from every conceivable direction.

Maybe you're fighting a battle. Maybe some major disappointment has dealt you a severe blow. You're tired and stressed out. You're flirting with the idea of giving up. You're at the quitting point. The quitting point is the point of utter exhaustion, overwhelming disappointment, and unexplainable weakness. It's the point of greatest discouragement.

Often you feel like you're running a long, dark marathon, unable to see where you're going. You feel like your heart will break and that your legs will collapse. "Where is the finish line?" you cry. "*Is* there a finish line?"

For you, there might be a thousand legitimate reasons to quit. Right now, it seems right and logical. Everyone else is quitting, so why not? Why go on? Why try?

No one is exempt from discouragement and fatigue. Every person—whether a runner, student, dieter, athlete, eacher, minister, spouse, parent, or disease victim—reaches a quitting point at some time or another.

Every day in our world, more than 1,000 people quit on life, choosing suicide as an escape from their hurts and fears. Each day, 9,000 others try and fail. One teenager attempts suicide every second! Suicide is a modern-day reality. Why? Because hope has been lost. Broken homes, unsatisfying relationships, bad marriages, shattered dreams, terminal illness, unemployment, and financial distress push people to the quitting point.

If you're ready to quit, understand one thing: Suicide is *not* an option!

Listen to God's Word: "Let us not become weary in doing good, for at the proper time we will reap a harvest if we do not give up" (Gal. 6:9 NIV). Starters abound, but stickers and finishers are a rare breed. Although multitudes defect, don't be weary in your race, your fight, your studies, your marriage, your ministry. Hang tough and go the distance! It's always too soon to quit. There's little to gain by quitting, but much to lose.

In the pages that follow, you will find the necessary encouragement, hope, and spiritual strength to carry you beyond the simple stress points and the major quitting points of your life.

2

Agony in the Arena

The hill of agony produces the greatest athletes and the school of affliction produces the greatest scholars!

In Kenya, there is a hill that the Kenyans have named the "hill of agony." This hill provides a steep, agonizing course for Kenyan runners to train on, resulting in the development of their tremendous strength and stamina. It's no wonder that Kenya has produced so many world-class runners and gold medal winners over the years: Champions are often born in the heat of agony and adversity.

Agony and anguish in life are unavoidable. Pain is a universal problem. Hebrews 12:1 (NIV) challenges us to "run with perseverance the race marked out for us." The Greek word translated "race" is the word *agonia*, which depicts a grueling and demanding struggle. It is also the word from which the English words *agony* and *anguish* are derived.

Christianity is not a picnic, party, or playground; it's a race. And in this race, miles are not always counted as units of joy, but sometimes as units of agony. When you come to Christ, you enter a new arena of activity; the new birth is just the starting line. Those of us who have been in this arena for long can assure you that affliction and adversity, heartache and heartbreak, are realities in this race. Like it or not, pain is part of the program. Paul and Barnabas, preaching to new Christians, exhorted, "We must through many tribulations enter the kingdom of God" (Acts 14:22b).

Dear friends, do not be surprised at the painful trial you are suffering, as though something strange were happening to you (1 Peter 4:12 NIV).

Too many have been deceived into believing that Christianity is an easy downhill jog to the finish line. When problems, pain, and pressure arise, people don't know how to cope, and they quit. How tragic! Unfortunately, sometimes Christianity is "pie in the face" rather than "pie in the sky."

In Second Corinthians 4:8-9, Paul describes himself as being "hard pressed...perplexed...persecuted...struck down." In Second Corinthians 7:5, he states that "our bodies had no rest, but we were troubled on every side. Outside were conflicts, inside were fears." In Second Corinthians 11:23-28, he talks about labors, scourgings, prisons, deaths, beatings with rods, stonings, shipwrecks, long stressful journeys, perils, weariness, sleeplessness, hunger, thirst, cold, and nakedness—plus the taxing care of all the churches. And in Second Corinthians 4:17, he refers to all of this as "light affliction."

Wow! No one had more legitimate reason to quit than did Paul, but he stood firm, fought the good fight, and finished the race.

For every Christian, there is a "hill of agony" designed to qualify us for future ministries and rewards. Trials and tough times are necessary, working for our good and completion. Every heartache and hardship must be treated as part of the training necessary to make you a champion. As Romans 8:28 says, "And we know that all things work together for good to those who love God, to those who are the called according to His purpose." And Second Corinthians 4:17 assures us that our affliction is working for us.

Isn't it marvelous how the very things that cause us pain are actually working for our benefit?

Not only are our trials beneficial, but they are also only temporary—"but for a moment," according to Second Corinthians 4:17. While comforting the persecuted church of the first century, Peter states, "Now for a little while, if need be, you have been grieved by various trials" (1 Pet. 1:6b).

Hebrews 12:1 (NIV) describes the race as already being marked out for us. The course you are running, as well as its degree of difficulty, is not of your own choosing but of God's. His job is to lay the course out for you, and your only job is to run it. Because everything in your course has been sovereignly surveyed by God, you can rest assured that you will face nothing that cannot work toward your ultimate and eternal good. Everything that touches us has already been approved by God. Remembering this will help you endure each trial and finish the race.

Remember, we are not merely called to run the race. Anyone can run, but according to First Corinthians 9:24, we are called to finish and to win! We are destined to be conquerors, not just survivors. We are more than conquerors! (See Romans 8:37.)

3

Heartbreak Hill

Heartbreak is not meant to defeat us, but to deepen and develop us!

Mile 20! I'm running the prestigious Boston Marathon. More than 7,000 runners came to the starting line. By now, several hundred have already dropped out.

Those of us still running must now face our greatest test: Heartbreak Hill. The real challenge actually begins at mile 13, with a series of hills that climax at mile 20 with the formidable and notorious Heartbreak Hill.

A half-mile long, Heartbreak Hill is extremely steep and grueling. At this point, I am spent! Drained! I have given all that I had to give. Utter exhaustion has overtaken my senses; unexplainable weakness has set in. Everything of nutritional, energy-producing value has burned up. My legs do not want to cooperate, my vision is blurred, and I'm rapidly losing my orientation.

I'm already at the quitting point.

For years, I've heard about Heartbreak Hill, and now finally we meet. As I look at the hill, I realize that I have already struggled 19 hard miles to get here. Can I make it any further? Am I equal to this supreme test?

I want to negotiate with that hill. "Be reasonable; treat me gently. Don't be too hard on me!" But I soon realize that Heartbreak Hill has no favorites and is no respecter of persons. It is gentle on no one; and if you do not beat it, it will beat you. You must conquer it, or it will conquer you! For 100 years, ever since the first Boston Marathon, even many of the world's most elite runners have been victims of Heartbreak Hill—not to mention those who were unprepared, untrained, or undisciplined.

There is no way to avoid Heartbreak Hill—no shortcuts or easy ways to reach the finish line seven miles away in downtown Boston. To get to the finish line of this 26.2 mile route, each runner has to go over Heartbreak Hill.

Christianity is also a marathon. It's an endurance course. Along the route there are numerous hills, many of which are difficult and demanding. And somewhere along the way, every Christian encounters one hill more demanding than the rest—the supreme test of his character.

Heartbreak Hill is real! Although heartache and hardship are unavoidable, they are not designed to cripple us, but to complete us. Heartbreak is not meant to defeat us, but to deepen and develop us and to eventually bring us to the glorious finish line of life.

God's business is making men. He is more concerned about character than comfort, faith than feelings. True Christian character can only be produced at the expense of comfort. Most of us have become so comfort-oriented that we resist the slightest bit of discomfort. Some have even been taught that anything that disrupts our comfort is not of God. Nothing could be any further from the truth! God often permits discomfort in order to produce character:

> *Blessed is the man who perseveres under trial, because when he has stood the test, he will receive the crown of life...* (James 1:12 NIV).

At Heartbreak Hill, you have the choice to pout and protest or pray and persevere. Maybe you're there right now and some difficulty is threatening to break and devastate you. Never forget that difficulties are not impossibilities! With God, all things are possible. In fact, He specializes in things thought impossible. You can beat this heartache. You can conquer this hill of hardship. You can do all things through Christ who continually pours His power into you (see Phil. 4:13). Press on, my friend! Rest but don't quit! Bend, but don't break! You've come too far to stop now.

With the generous support of an encouraging crowd (see Chapter 17, "Crowd Support"), I was able to conquer Heartbreak Hill. Six miles later, I turned left onto Boylston Street in downtown Boston, with only a half-mile left to the finish line. What a feeling! To finish a marathon is the ultimate achievement in long-distance running.

Somewhere beyond the heartbreaks and hardships of life, there is a finish line complete with rewards and divine recognition. Don't stop short! Don't quit during the tough times! Go the distance and claim your reward!

4

Stickers Versus Quitters

Winners are never quitters, and quitters are never winners!

Velcro is a universal fastener, invented in 1948 by a Swiss engineer inspired by the seed burrs sticking to his socks after a field walk. It is now used on everything from clothes and shoes to pipeline insulation to keeping things in place (including astronauts on a space shuttle).

Nylon filament is the base material most often used to weave velcro, which emerges from the loom as a fabric with an intensely loopy nap. The loop-tops on some of the fabric are clipped, producing a forest of small, stiff hooks. When placed against the loops of the unclipped fabric, these hooks will grasp with amazing tenacity. It takes 10-15 pounds of force per square inch to separate standard velcro.[1]

The world's population can be divided into two categories: *stickers* and *quitters*. As we live, we develop a track record. Take a good look at your track record. How does it read? Has quitting become habitual with you? How do you react to pressure? How do you respond to adversity?

---

1. Adapted from *The Academic American Encyclopedia*, Vol. 19 (Grolier Inc., 1996), 537.

Our society possesses a dropout, "take the easy way out" mentality.

- Over 300,000 husbands and over 600,000 wives quit on their marriages each year in America.

- Nearly 3,000 teenagers run away from home each day.

- Forty-five percent of young people between the ages of 12 and 18 drop out of church.

- Only four percent (1 in 25) of those entering the ministry at age 21 are still in the ministry at age 65. The other 96 percent drop out over the years.

Quitting often disguises itself in other terms and forms (i.e., drop out, backslide, divorce, run away, resign, etc.). We could be called the "drop-out generation" or the "run-away society." Multitudes have deserted their posts, families, jobs, churches, studies, diets, and fitness programs. We've become a generation of quitters, rather than stickers! The average church contains deserted pews, altars, Sunday school rooms, and pulpits.

Almost everywhere I go, I hear people say, "I wish I could just run away from it all." We cringe when the heat rises. We cry, "I'm out of here!" at the slightest problem.

The marriage has gone stale. You're stressed out by the children. You're bored and restless in your life. Each day seems more unbearable. You wonder, "Is it worth staying?"

The pressures of raising a family in such a complex society are frightening. You're trying to juggle the work schedule, family activity, church responsibilities, household chores, and a fitness program. It's an uphill battle. You wonder, "Why not just run away from it all?"

The house is nice, you have two cars in the garage, a large screen TV, a comfortable lifestyle, many friends, and financial security—but no happiness. Instead, there is only a painful, lingering emptiness. The romance is over. The magic is gone. "Why stick it out?" you wonder. "Why pretend? Isn't divorce the fashionable way to deal with marital unhappiness?"

Your heart is broken! Teenage pregnancy can be the most cruel, traumatic experience of a young person's life. Your boyfriend's promises were empty, and his love for you was nothing more than lust. You feel worthless, cheated, and hurt. You wonder, "How can I face another day? How can I live with such pain? Is there really anything to live for?"

The church is on the decline. There is a negative undercurrent affecting your reputation. Last night's board meeting was agonizing. The leaders have threatened to cut your salary if finances don't improve. You wonder, "Is this what serving God is all about?" At times like this, resigning seems best. You consider, "I'm just a failure, so why go on?"

There are times when even the strongest, most faithful Christian reaches the quitting point. His soul is plunged into the depths of discouragement and despair. Everything seems to be going wrong. There seems to be no end to the problems. The urge to run intensifies.

At a certain quitting point in his life, the psalmist David cried out,

> ...Oh, that I had wings like a dove! I would fly away and be at rest. ... I would hasten my escape from the windy storm and tempest (Psalm 55:6,8).

But for every problem, there is a problem solver. His name is Jesus. Don't run from your problems. Instead, run to the Problem Solver. When life is at its worst, Christ is always at His best. When many of His disciples were running away and forsaking Him, Jesus turned to the 12 and asked, "Will you run away too, like the others?" Peter answered Him, "Lord, to whom shall we go? You have the words of eternal life." (See John 6:66-68.)

Something needs to be said about sticking, staying put, and standing firm despite the pressure. My high school track coach often reminded us that "winners are never quitters, and quitters are never winners." Winners are stickers; losers are quitters. Winners possess a velcro-like tenacity that refuses to let go even during times of great disappointment, injury, or loss.

Starting and sticking are two different things. Anybody can start, but few can stick.

- Everybody goes to kindergarten, but few earn diplomas, and even fewer earn degrees.

- Millions start diets and fitness programs, but few follow through and lose the desired weight.

- Thousands start marathons. Few ever see the finish line.

- Multitudes get married. Only about 50 percent stick.

Let's see...how many repair jobs have you started recently? And how many have you finished? Get my drift?

Something needs to be said about finding the center of God's will and staying put regardless of the stress or pain involved. Something needs to be said about velcro-like "stick-to-it"-iveness. There are just too many divorced couples, broken homes, and split churches—all resulting from a lack of "stick-ability" and the inability to ride out the storms and persevere through problems. Falling in love is easy; anyone can fall in love. Staying in love is where the difficulty comes in. Sticking together through thick and thin is no easy task; it requires much patience.

Quit is a nasty four letter word. Let me encourage you to be a sticker and not a quitter. Stick to the Lord! Stick to your family! Stick to the Bible! Stick to God's plan for your life! Stick to a full-gospel church! Stick to your convictions!

Stick even when you learn that your husband is leaving you for another woman. Stick even when the doctor announces the dreaded news that you have a terminal illness. Stick even when your teenage daughter shocks you with the words, "Mom? Dad? I'm pregnant." Stick even when the state police calls to inform you that your son was killed while driving under the influence of alcohol. Stick and don't quit even if all hell breaks out against you. Stick and finish the course. We'll talk more about how to "stick" later.

Review the following contrast to determine whether you're a quitter or a sticker:

Quitter: "It may be possible, but I think it's too difficult."
Sticker: "It may be difficult, but I think it's possible."

Quitter: "That's not my job!"
Sticker: "Let me do it!"

Quitter: Always sees the sand trap next to the green.
Sticker: Always sees the green next to the sand trap.

Quitter: Always has an excuse.
Sticker: Always has a plan.

Quitter: Always becomes a part of the problem.
Sticker: Always becomes a part of the solution.

Quitter: "I can't and you can't, so let's give up!"
Sticker: "I can and you can, so let's go for it."

What conclusion did you draw?

The Bible is a catalog containing the resumés of both quitters and stickers. In the upcoming chapters, we'll examine the lives of some to find out what made them stick or quit.

5

The Sixth Time: Stubborn Walls

Victory, reward, and the satisfying sense of fulfillment come only to those who stick and refuse to quit.

The sun was just beginning to rise on the eastern horizon when Joshua gave the command to move out. Suddenly the parade was underway. Forty thousand soldiers began to march, followed by seven priests carrying seven trumpets, followed by the Ark of the Covenant, followed by a rearguard. God had promised victory at Jericho. For the promise to be fulfilled, absolute obedience would be required.

In Joshua chapter 6, we find that God had a special strategy for conquering the city of Jericho. The plan involved a peculiar-looking procession consisting of soldiers, priests, and a four-foot by two-foot by two-foot wooden box. Around the city they marched. After the first circuit was completed, they stopped and rested the remainder of the day. This procedure continued for six straight days.

On the seventh day, however, there was no rest in the action. Once the command was given, the company continued marching. One lap. Two. Three. Four. Five. Six. At first, everything had been great. Excitement was high; faith was strong. With each additional day and each additional lap, however, came more weariness and discouragement. By the sixth time around on the seventh day, I suspect that Joshua and his troops were at the quitting point. Incredible doubt and despair were setting in. This was their first experience with stubborn walls of opposition.

You see, some thought the walls would fall on Monday. Others predicted Wednesday. Some suggested the walls would fall after one lap around. Others expected the collapse to take place after three laps. When the walls didn't fall, those with preconceived notions became quickly discouraged.

There's a big problem with trying to predict God. There's a great danger in trying to put God on a schedule or fit Him into a time table. To do so usually means to set yourself up for major disappointment. With God, the walls don't always fall on Wednesday or on Friday. Growth doesn't always come in the third year of a pastorate. Healing doesn't always occur the first time you're anointed and prayed for.

God commanded, "Start marching! Blow the trumpets! Leave the walls and the timing to me." Joshua and the children of Israel were only to be obedient, and they needed to leave the details and timing to God. God was saying, "You march, and I'll take care of your walls and your giants. Do what you can do and I'll do the rest."

Why not leave the walls of your prison and your circumstances to God? Begin in humble obedience to do what you can do. Pray, trust, and God will do what you can't do: He'll take care of your walls and your giants.

Remember that God is a specialist when it comes to walls, whether they're legal walls, insurmountable walls of tradition, or walls of misunderstanding. Formidable walls of fear and doubt, financial walls, family walls, denominational walls, heart walls, church walls—God still does walls, even stubborn, Jericho-like walls!

Walls are dividers that restrict progress and hinder victory. Furthermore, they form strongholds in which the enemy can dwell. Some walls are self-erected. Others are established by the enemy. I personally believe that satan and his demons infiltrate every city and church and erect walls and strongholds just like Jericho's.

Archaeologists tell us that Jericho's wall was actually a double wall. The two walls were about 15 feet apart and linked together by houses built across the top. The outer wall was 6 feet thick; the inner wall, 12 feet thick. Both were about 30 feet high. Jericho's walls were formidable, insurmountable, and unconquerable. The city itself was a symbol of military power and strength, and the Canaanites considered it invincible.

Let's go back to that seventh day and the sixth time around. Can you get a feel for the mood of this company? It wasn't your typical upbeat, positive mood. The atmosphere reeked with skepticism and pessimism.

"This is absolutely ridiculous," some suggested. Others complained, "We're tired! We've been going through this ridiculous ritual for seven days, and not even one lousy stone has fallen." Some protested, "We're making complete fools of ourselves. These walls ain't gonna fall!" Someone even dared to accuse Joshua of missing God. "Boy, have you missed it this time, brother."

Don't you know Joshua and company had had it? I mean, not even one stone had become dislodged. All the marching and blowing of trumpets had been for nothing. There was absolutely no visible indication that the walls would fall.

This Jericho experience was a long, drawn-out ordeal. Most Bible scholars estimate that the path around the city was approximately 1.5 miles long—not an exhaustive distance, until you multiply it by 13. They circled the city one time for six days (9.0 miles). Then on the seventh day, they circled the city seven times (10.5 miles). All told, they marched seven days for a total of 13 laps (19.5 miles)! I know exactly what you are thinking: Why couldn't God devise a nice, little, easy, instant plan for the walls to come down? Why seven days and 13 laps?

Let me suggest that faith and character have to be tested. In the mechanical world, everything gets tested, from the smallest needle to the largest engine. In fact, as a product's value is increased, the test becomes more severe. Whatever passes the test is stamped with a trademark and marketed. Whatever fails the test is rejected. Believe it or not, time is the greatest tester of all, which means that for every promise there must be a corresponding delay. Nothing tests the quality of a person's character quite like time does.

I suspect that these are testing times for you, your family, or maybe even your church. Perhaps, just as with Jericho, this is the fifth or sixth time you've been around the wall. Why the delay? Why no answer or miracle? Why no victory or apparent growth? Why aren't your walls coming down?

Perhaps God is testing your obedience, commitment, perseverance, or faith. Will you be absolutely obedient although you see no indication of a miracle? Will you continue to serve God even if He doesn't show up by Friday? Will you continue to trust even if you don't experience healing after the sixth prayer meeting? Learn to rejoice in every test. Why? Because the test is for your good. What sort of maker or manufacturer would market a product that had not first been tested? God is going to use you, but first He must test you.

We all know what happened on the seventh day, after the seventh time Israel marched around Jericho: The stubborn walls came tumbling down. At first they looked immovable, but God was faithful and brought them down, just as He had promised Joshua.

Our primary concern, however, is with the sixth lap on the seventh day. It must have been the most despairing of all. The temptation to give up must have been powerful. This must have been their quitting point.

Have you felt like quitting lately? Is the pressure getting to you? Have you lost your joy? It's easy to shout when the walls are down; it's easy to sing in the shower, but can we sing in the jailhouse? Can we shout while the walls are standing and the enemy is threatening?

For your marriage or your ministry, this may be the sixth time. All you may have known is despair and defeat. Be encouraged! Because days of disappointment and despair often precede days of victory and blessing.

Jericho's walls represent anything that appears unconquerable, unmovable, or insurmountable. Have you noticed that most walls are stubborn walls? Habits can be like walls—stubborn and unwilling to move. Unforgiveness can loom high like a Jericho wall. Financial debt can appear insurmountable. Apathy and hypocrisy can seem rather intimidating. Marital misunderstanding can emerge as a modern-day Jericho right in your own home.

Are you intimidated by the stronghold? Does a breakthrough seem beyond your reach? Let me encourage you to commit every offensive and dividing wall to God. You're no match for the dividing walls of hate and prejudice, misunderstanding, and unforgiveness. "Commit your way to the Lord, trust also in Him, and He shall bring it to pass" (Ps. 37:5). The walls may loom great, high and thick, discouraging and despairing, but God looms greater! Don't fear the walls of discord and doubt! Don't fear the satanic strongholds of pride and rebellion! Through persistent faith and prayer, every hindering and dividing wall will come down.

Joshua's success at Jericho had nothing to do with the battle conditions. The height and thickness of the walls, as well as the enemy's strength, were inconsequential. This victory occurred because of obedience and perseverance. Had Joshua and company stopped short of absolute obedience, there would have never been a victory. So keep marching and blowing your trumpet! Keep praying and claiming the promises of God. By and by, in God's time, when the time is right, the walls will come down. And great will be your breakthrough!

"Breakthrough" is always the result of "breakdown." Jericho's walls need to be broken down before God's people can break through and claim the victory. (See Joshua 6:20.)

6

The Sixth Time: Nothing at All?

Faith is the ability to hold fast when all you can see is nothing.

It was an exhausting ordeal. Elijah had called the bluff of 850 Baal-worshiping cronies, called fire from Heaven, led Israel into revival, and finally had all 850 false prophets slain with the sword. With the victory now secure, surely God would send the promised rain.

Three-and-one-half years had passed since the last rain. Israel was experiencing the most devastating drought in her history. There was not even a cloud in the sky. Nonetheless, Elijah predicted rain, informing King Ahab, "There is the sound of abundance of rain" (1 Kings 18:41b).

If you make a statement like this on a sunny, cloudless morning, you'd better have a word from the Lord. Elijah did: God had promised him, "Go, present yourself to Ahab, and I will send rain on the earth" (1 Kings 18:1b).

Maybe God has promised you healing, a marriage miracle, or the salvation of a loved one, but there is not even the slightest hint of fulfillment. What do you do when you have a promise and word from God, but nothing is happening that would indicate that an answer or solution is forthcoming? Elijah did three things: He *pressed on higher*, *prostrated himself*, and *persistently prayed* (see 1 Kings 18:42).

After a season of prayer, Elijah sent his servant to a high point and commanded him to look toward the sea. After a prolonged gaze, the servant returned to inform Elijah, "There is nothing" (1 Kings 18:43). How depressing! I can't think of any more disheartening words. All that praying and believing for nothing. What do you do when your prayers are not answered and it appears God is not coming through for you? Let me suggest that you do precisely what Elijah did. He prayed again.

He sent his servant a second time, and then a third, a fourth, a fifth, and a sixth. Each time the servant returned with the same negative answer: "Nothing!" This happened six times in a row.

Have you ever looked for a positive sign only to be disappointed by a negative one? Perhaps you go to the mailbox expecting the promised funds you need to silence a belligerent creditor, but *nothing* is there.

You go to the doctor for your scheduled appointment, confidently expecting a good report, only to be devastated by the news that *nothing* about your condition has changed.

You wait anxiously by the phone, anticipating an invitation to sing, preach, or teach, only to see another day pass with no opportunity presented.

According to James 5:17, "Elijah was a man with a nature like ours...." He was subject to the same fears and frustrations as you and me. His heart sank with each negative report, and his spirit grieved with each painful delay. He probably questioned, "Why bother? What's the use?"

Elijah was at the quitting point. Six times he prayed, and six times he was met with disappointment. Six times he looked for an answer only to find *nothing*. Yet he never gave up: Overwhelmed by exhaustion, he kept praying.

To pray again simply means to persist in prayer. To pray a second time or a third is not a sign of disbelief, but one of great faith. It means that you really do believe that what God has promised, He is able to perform. Jesus encouraged us to persevere:

Keep on asking and it will be given you; keep on seeking and you will find; keep on knocking [reverently] and [the door] will be opened to you. For everyone who keeps on asking receives; and he who keeps on seeking finds; and to him who keeps on knocking, [the door] will be opened (Matthew 7:7-8 AMP).

E.M. Bounds one of the greatest authorities on the subject of prayer, declared, "Jesus taught that perseverance is the essential element of prayer... Too ofter we get fainthearted and quit praying at the point where we ought to begin. We let go at the very point where we should hold on strongest. Our prayers are weak becasue they are not impassioned by an unfailing and resistless will."[1]

George Muller once wrote, "The great point is never to give up until the answer comes. I have been praying for sixty-three years and eight months for one man's conversion. He is not saved yet, but he will be. How can it be otherwise? ...I am praying." Muller's friend eventually received Christ—on the very day that Muller's casket was lowered into the ground. There, near the open grave, this friend surrendered his life to Christ.

Most people today are looking for easy solutions, quick fixes, and simple formulas. Persistence in prayer is a lost art. Stop trying to think it through or reason it through. Pray it through. Too often, we get through praying before we pray through.

---

1. E.M. Bounds, Purpose in Prayer (Westwood, NJ: The Christian Library, 1984), 50.

Elijah finally said to his servant, "Go again!" In this text, we see the beauty of teamwork. This servant is burned out as well; Elijah's been doing the kneework, but the servant's been doing the legwork. He must have protested, "Again? Boss, you must be crazy! I've already looked six times. There's nothing there!" But Elijah pleaded, "Just once more. We can't give up. God has promised!"

We know what happened the seventh time. A cloud was spotted in the western sky. It was small, just the size of a man's hand. But then, within minutes, the entire sky was black with clouds, and there was a torrential downpour (1 Kings 18:44-45). It all happened just as God had promised!

Maybe you've also looked for the sixth time and have reached your quitting point. You've been looking for healing, restoration, finances, or revival. You've prayed and believed but received nothing—no sign, no indication that God's listening, no cloud on the horizon. Let me encourage you to look again. There is nothing gained by quitting. Faith is the ability to hold fast when all you see nothing. Faith is holding-on power. Faith may not keep your husband from running out or sickness from afflicting your body, but it will give you the strength to hold on. Faith doesn't always alter the circumstances, but it always anchors the Christian!

Dear friend, if God has promised and given assurance, then don't lose heart. A cloud will soon appear. And when it does, never be discouraged by its size; the downpour that follows will be abundantly greater than your mind could imagine.

7

The Sixth Time:
Muddy Waters

The only thing worse than quitting is never beginning.

He was a popular national hero, a brilliant military strategist who had delivered his country from many enemies. A man of great honor, courage, and reputation, whose clothing bore all the appropriate military regalia that signified rank and his many accomplishments. He was the captain of the Syrian army, and his name was Naaman.

Despite his rank, popularity, and many deeds, Naaman was a desperate helpless leper. Leprosy was the most dreaded disease of his day. Incurable. Leprosy was so deadly that it overshadowed all the success of one's life. People who contracted it were usually shunned from society, regardless of their past achievements. Because of his leprosy, it didn't matter how popular, prosperous, or powerful the captain had become. The death shadow hovered over his life.

During a certain battle, a Jewish girl was taken captive and eventually became a servant to Naaman's wife. This girl often told stories of the great prophet Elisha, and one day she suggested that if only Naaman could have an audience with Elisha, he could be cured of his leprosy.

Naaman, desperate for a cure, prepared for the journey. He took along 10 talents of silver, 6,000 pieces of gold, and 10 new suits of clothing. Apparently he was prepared to buy his healing. He soon discovered, however, that the thing that he needed most could not be gained by political clout or bought with gold. Naaman had to realize that God's cure was a free gift.

When Elisha heard of Naaman's arrival in Israel, he said, "Please let him come to me, and he shall know that there is a prophet in Israel" (2 Kings 5:8b). Talk about faith!

Naaman pulled up with his entourage in one of the hottest-looking chariots of that day. Surely the man of God would be impressed, but Elisha didn't flinch or even respond. He didn't greet Naaman, nor did he invite him in for a glass of refreshing iced tea, or anoint him with oil, or lay hands upon him and pray a prayer of faith. He didn't even anoint a handkerchief and send it out to be laid upon the sick captain.

As Naaman stood at Elisha's door, impatiently knocking, a servant came out with the following instructions: "Go and wash in the Jordan seven times, and your flesh shall be restored to you, and you shall be clean" (2 Kings 5:10b).

Naaman became furious. His pride was wounded. What an insult to his rank and dignity! Didn't Elisha realize who he was? As though being denied an audience with Elisha wasn't bad enough, he was then told to wash in the muddy Jordan River. The text specifically says that he "turned and went away in a rage" (2 Kings 5:12). Not having gotten his own way, Naaman stormed off.

But Naaman's servants were able to convince him to at least give it a shot. What else would he have to lose but his pride?

As it turned out, Naaman had been hoping to dictate the terms of his healing, but God Himself had determined the way. If the muddy Jordan River indicates anything, it's that the way to salvation, healing, and revival is never dignified.

If you really want something from God, you must be willing to die to your pride and just obey.

Naaman reluctantly obeyed, which, in my eyes, was better than no obedience at all. (After all, I'd prefer that my children reluctantly obey me rather than defy my authority altogether.) He waded out into the river and dipped himself.

One time. "How stupid!" he thought.

Two times. "Surely I'm making a fool out of myself," he grumbled.

Three times. "I must look like a complete idiot," he complained.

Four times. "I have my pride!" he muttered.

Five times. "What a ridiculous ritual!" he protested.

Six times. "What a waste! There is absolutely no improvement. If anything, I look worse. Why trust in God?"

Naaman had reached a quitting point, after having gone through the exercise six times with absolutely no indication of a miracle. Maybe you've been down numerous times with no visible sign of a miracle either. The sixth time is the time of greatest despair. The time just before the miracle is when you'll experience the strongest temptation to quit.

But Naaman was desperate. He didn't just want healing; he wanted it more than anything else in life. And, when Naaman went down for the seventh time, suddenly and miraculously his flesh was restored. The leprosy vanished. He was healed.

Perhaps you're being humbled by a Jordan River in your life. The experience is a blow to your pride. But for you, like Naaman, this is your last resort. You've tried everything else. You've got nothing to lose. You've been to the doctors looking for a cure, the lawyers looking for a solution, the counselors looking for an answer, and the banks looking for credit. It's time to stand on God's word: Die to your pride and trust in God for your miracle!

When you reach your quitting point, stay in the river. Stay at the altar! Keep trusting and praying. When God says "seven times," make sure you don't stop at six. Six won't do! Don't stop short of complete obedience.

How many times have we given up too soon? Perhaps we have failed to persist in what God had asked us to do—one more time forward, one more prayer meeting, five more minutes at the altar—and the miracle would have happened.

The secret to obtaining great things from God lies in perseverance. Most quitting takes place after the sixth time down, during the last half hour, or right before the break of dawn. If God has called you to an act of obedience, then your miracle depends on your obedience to His Word and your perseverance in His will. Hang tough, and God will be faithful.

8

Perseverance:
The Winning Ingredient

Too often we get through praying before we pray through.

Weary to the point of exhaustion, men working with Thomas Edison sighed, "What a waste! We've tried 700 experiments, and nothing has happened. We're no better off than when we began."

"Oh yes we are," Edison responded. "We now know 700 things that won't work. That means that we're closer than we've ever been before." And with an optimistic twinkle in his eye, he rolled up his sleeves and proceeded to invent the light bulb.

That's perseverance.

Edison was the world's most tenacious inventor. He was also the world's greatest experimenter. He was known to try thousands and thousands of ways—sometimes 50,000—to do a thing, and he kept trying, even if it was to take ten years. According to Edison, the three greatest essentials to achieve anything worthwhile are perseverance, hard work, and common sense.

Edison worked harder and slept less than any other great man in history. While perfecting the phonograph, he once worked continuously for five days and nights without any sleep. He conducted more experiments than any other human being. In his lifetime, he secured a grand total of over 1,000 patents—a number unapproached by any other individual in history. No one has added more to the comfort and enjoyment of life than Edison.

Difficulties that would drive normal people to despair only lit up Edison's enthusiasm and stimulated his determination to triumph. He repeatedly lost all his money and encountered bitter defeat. But even in the face of failure, he cheerfully replied, "Our work has not been in vain; our experiments have taught us a lot. We have added something to the total of human knowledge: We have demonstrated that it can't be done."

That was Edison. He never wasted time bemoaning past failures while the future was calling so loudly for great accomplishments. A minister once asked him, "What is the greatest safeguard against temptation?" Reportedly, Edison replied, "If I were to hazard a guess as to what young people should do to avoid temptation, it would be to get a job and work at it so hard that temptation would not exist for them."

Edison stretched out his hand, seized hold of the fleeting sounds of the human voice, and made them imperishable by means of the recording machine. He captured motion with his invention of moving pictures, helped send sound across continents by his achievements in telephony, and (most important of all) flooded our world with electric light. Not only did Edison leave us a legacy of material conveniences but he also left a legacy in the value of perseverance, dedication, and determination.[1]

---

1. Adapted from "Thomas Edison," by B.C. Forbes in *Of America*, Vol. 1 (Pensacola, FL: A Beka Book Publications, 1985), 34-37.

Somebody Said It Couldn't Be Done

Somebody said it couldn't be done,
       But he, with a chuckle, replied
That maybe it couldn't, but he would be one
       Who wouldn't say so till he'd tried.

He waded right in with a trace of a grin
       On his face—if he worried, he hid it,
He started to sing as he tackled the thing
       That couldn't be done—and he did it.

Somebody said, "Oh, you'll never do that,
       At least no one ever has done it."
But he took off his coat and he took off his hat
       And the first thing we knew, he'd begun it.

With a lift of the chin and a bit of a grin
       Without any doubting or "quit it,"
He started to sing as he tackled the thing
       That couldn't be done—and he did it.

There are thousands to tell you it cannot be done,
       There are thousands to prophesy failure,
There are thousands to point out to you, one by one,
       The dangers that wait to assail you.

But just buckle in with a lift of the chin,
       Take off your coat and go to it,
Starting to sing as you tackle the thing
       That cannot be done—and you'll do it.[2]

The ability to stick and not quit—to keep on keeping on—is called perseverance. The Greek word translated as "patience" or "perserverance" is the word *hupomone*. It's the ability to triumphantly prevail and the power to cheerfully endure. It's the fiber that keeps you at task and on track. It's the winning ingredient!

---

2.   Edgar A. Guest, *Of America*, Vol. 1 (Pensacola, FL: A Beka Book Publications, 1984), 81.

We are encouraged in Hebrews to "run with perseverance the race marked out for us" (Heb. 12:1 NIV). Hebrews 10:36 reveals one of our greatest spiritual needs: "For you have need of endurance [perseverance], so that after you have done the will of God you may receive the promise [what has been promised]". Without perseverance, you can't succeed, achieve, or finish. Without it, you'll quit on your marriage, your family, church, studies, and ministry.

Perseverance Gets You From the Promise to the Fulfillment

For every promise there is a corresponding delay. A *delay* is the period of time between the delivery (or announcement) of the promise and the fulfillment of the promise. Delays vary in time. They can be very short or (as we all know) they can be painfully long.

No doubt, the greatest reason to hang tough and stick is the promised prize. If you quit, you forfeit the promise and the prize. In no race do they hand out awards to the starters; only those who stick and finish become candidates for the awards. In each of the ten marathons and scores of shorter races that I've run, I was tempted to quit. On a few occasions, I did. It didn't take me long to discover that victory, reward, and the satisfying sense of fulfillment come only to those who stick and refuse to quit.

Before you can receive the promise or the promised prize, you must persevere in doing the will of God. Notice the word *after* in Hebrews 10:36. The promised miracle or ministry comes after you persevere, not before. No perseverance, no prize! It's just that simple. If you quit, you forfeit the promise. If you stop doing the will of God, you disqualify yourself from receiving the promise and blessing of God. All the promises of God hinge on obedient perseverance. Remember Joshua at Jericho? Naaman in the Jordan?

Failure to patiently persevere can also short-circuit the entire plan of God for your life. One thing I've discovered is that God is rarely early, but He's never late. The words of this obscure Negro spiritual may be an encouragement to you.

> *You can't hurry God, oh no,*
> *   you just have to wait.*
> *You've got to trust Him and give Him time*
> *   no matter how long it takes.*
> *Well, He's God that you can't hurry,*
> *   but He'll be there, so don't you worry.*
> *Well, He may not come when you want Him,*
> *   but He's right on time.*[3]

Remember Abraham? When he was 75 years old, God promised him a son. For 11 years, Abe trusted God. Then at the age of 86, unhappy with the progress being made, Abe decided he would help God out. Big mistake! The end result was disastrous. It not only set God's plan back another 14 years, but it resulted in generations of bloodshed and conflict (see Gen. 15–21).

Despite his temporary lapse of faith, Abraham did persevere. Hebrews 6:15 declares, "And so, after he had patiently endured, he obtained the promise." Again, notice the word *after*. He received after he persevered, not before—25 years of perseverance! Don't expect to receive until after you persevere.

> *But may the God of all grace, who called us to His eternal glory by Christ Jesus, **after** you have suffered a while, perfect, establish, strengthen, and settle you* (1 Peter 5:10).

Other examples in the Bible abound.

- Noah persevered 120 years building a boat (without a Black and Decker saw) before the promised flood came.

- Joseph persevered 13 years from the prophetic dream to its fulfillment.

---

3. "You Can't Hurry God," Author unknown.

- Moses persevered 40 years in the desert before he could become Israel's deliverer.

- Joshua persevered seven days, 13 laps, and nearly 20 miles before the promised collapse of Jericho took place.

- David persevered 15 years from the anointing to the throne.

- The 120 disciples persevered in prayer for ten long days before the promised Holy Spirit fell.

Although delays can be painfully long, be encouraged to know that what God has promised, He is able also to perform (see Rom. 4:21). So hang tough and don't quit on the promise. So often we come to the brink of the miracle and we quit. We stop believing. We stop praying. Maybe the following words to an old song will be an encouragement to you.

Don't Give Up

Don't give up on the brink of a miracle,
   Don't give up, God is still on the throne;
Don't give up on the brink of a miracle,
   Don't give up, remember you're not alone.[4]

Perseverance Secures Victory in Spiritual Warfare

Most battles are long, drawn-out affairs—thus the need to persevere in the fight. Victory and revival can only be secured through spiritual warfare.

As Christians, most of our fighting is done on our knees. In Ephesians 6, which describes the battle and the armor, we are commanded to pray, "...always with all prayer and supplication in the Spirit, being watchful to this end with all perseverance..." (Eph. 6:18). Perseverance is needed to pray through to victory, revival, healing, and miracles.

---

4.   Mike Atkins, "Don't Give Up," 1985.

The great A.W. Tozer once said, "Revivals are born after midnight." In other words, revival is born after the Church has engaged in a prolonged season of prayer. Sadly, most American churches don't even have prayer meetings or altar services, let alone extended ones. This, no doubt, explains the absence of victory and revival in many of our churches.

There is nothing that we start and then quit more than prayer. We repeatedly stop short of victory and revival because we quit on prayer. We quit going to prayer meetings, going to the altar, and having private prayer and devotional time. We could experience life-changing answers and glorious victories if we would just persevere in prayer. Let's repent of quitting in the arena of prayer and begin today to pray through!

There is no hurt that cannot be healed, no stubborn lust that cannot be subdued, no temptation that cannot be conquered, and no stronghold that cannot be brought down through persevering prayer. The parable of the aggressive and persistent widow is prefaced with these words: "Men always ought to pray and not lose heart [quit]" (Lk. 18:16b).

Receiving the infilling and enduing of the Holy Spirit requires prayer perseverance as well. Luke records Jesus' own experience: "...while He prayed, the heaven was opened. And the Holy Spirit descended..." (Lk. 3:21-22). The Holy Spirit came down to equip and empower Jesus as He persevered in prayer. This enduement became a pattern for all servants of God.

Acts 1:14 declares, "These all continued with one accord in prayer...." Then we see in Acts 2:4, "And then they were all filled with the Holy Spirit...." Note that the early disciples continued in prayer. They diligently persevered for ten days until the promised blessing came.

Jesus gave the directive, "Behold, I send the Promise of My Father upon you; but tarry in the city of Jerusalem until you are endued with power from on high" (Lk. 24:49). The key word is *until.*

The question is often asked, "How long should I wait and pray?" Jesus answered, "Until you are endued with power." To "tarry...until" simply means to not give up until the power arrives. In the early days of American Pentecostalism, many churches conducted tarrying meetings. Today we have "how to" seminars in which we attempt to teach people how to receive. "After they prayed...they were all filled with the Holy Spirit..." (Acts 4:31 NIV). Notice again the word *after.* Most spiritual experiences come after a season of prayer and not before.

There has always been an undeniable link between persevering prayer and victory, revival, and the baptism of the Holy Spirit. Paul testified, "I have fought the good fight" (2 Tim. 4:7a). The "good fight" is a persevering fight. Step into the ring and stay in the fight, making every punch count until victory is secured!

Perseverance Gets Us From Seed Time to Harvest

Every believer plays a vital part in the production of spiritual fruit. One plants; another waters. One fertilizes, another cultivates, and a third reaps. Perseverance is a virtue that every farmer must possess. Farmers are incredibly patient people. The time between planting and reaping can be exceedingly long—usually months—and you cannot rush the production of fruit. If you impatiently attempt to rush the harvest, you'll destroy it. Growth takes time. If you try to hurry the process, you'll kill the thing! Whoever heard of helping a plant grow by grabbing it and pulling on it?

James describes this thought clearly:

> *...See how the farmer waits for the precious fruit of the earth, waiting patiently for it until it receives the early and latter rain. You also be patient..."* (James 5:7-8).

My number one weakness is impatience. I recently read where the average person spends seven years of his life waiting.

What a waste! Check-out lines, red lights, amusement park lines, doctors' offices, restaurants, banks, gas stations. Add it up, and you'll see seven long years of doing nothing but waiting. But the best things in life come to those who wait.

Have you ever been to Disney World? On a busy day, you can wait up to two hours for a one-minute ride. What a joke! Have you ever been in New York City? If you get caught in rush hour traffic, it can take you up to two hours just to drive two miles.

The medical waiting room is the most dreadful of experiences. You have a 10:00 appointment, but you arrive early, hoping to be taken in sooner—not a chance! 10:15, 10:30, and you're still waiting...10:45...11:00...still waiting. Periodically the nurse comes out, and you just know it's your turn, only to be disappointed as she calls out another name. Time passes...11:15...11:20...and then finally at 11:30—after you've chewed your last fingernail and your blood pressure has gone sky high—your name is called. Oh! Ask me to do anything but wait!

A lady once approached her pastor and humbly asked, "Pastor, will you please pray that God will give me patience?" Her caring pastor laid his hands upon her and began to pray, "Dear God, I pray that You will send my sister tremendous tribulation." Before the pastor could finish his prayer, the woman interrupted him and said, "No, no, Pastor! I asked you to pray for patience." To which the pastor responded, "My good sister, the Bible says, 'Tribulation worketh patience.' " (See Romans 5:3 KJV.)

There are certain things in life that you have no control over. Recognizing and accepting that fact will not only help you keep your cool when the heat is on, but it will preserve your sanity as well. The farmer has absolutely no control over the elements. He does all that he can do, and then he must wait for the sun and the rain to do their jobs. Both of those things are vital for the harvest.

Whatever you do, don't become impatient and quit on the fruit! The process can be long and tedious, but if there has been a seed time, there will be a harvest. It's inevitable! Passionately do what you can do, and then patiently persevere for the sovereign intervention of God.

Patience is a form of perseverance. Therefore, "...Let us not grow weary while doing good, for in due season we shall reap if we do not lose heart" (Gal. 6:9)!

Perseverance Enables Us to Make It to the Finish Line

Jesus didn't say, "He who endures to the starting line," but "...He who endures to the end [the finish line] shall be saved" (Mt. 24:13). To obtain the prize of eternal life, you must persevere through times of difficulty, disappointment, and delay.

- Robert Frost labored 39 years without any notice or recognition before he sold his first volume. That's perseverance!

- Henry Ford made 871 models before he found the one with which he was satisfied. That's perseverance!

- Dan Jansen skated in three Olympics and failed to medal in seven races before he finally won a gold medal. That's perseverance!

Without perseverance, you'll quit on God. The world is full of backsliders—those who compromised their stand and eventually quit on God. I'm on a mission to lower the dropout rate. Too many start but never finish. Paul declared, "I have finished my race" (see 2 Tim. 4:7). You can finish your race as well.

9

Quititis:
The Quitting Disease

Quitting only compounds the pain and complicates the problem.

The sons of Ephraim were skilled archers and marksmen. At target practice, they were brilliant; but on the battlefield, when the pressure was on, they retreated. Like foxes being hunted by hounds, they ran scared.

Psalm 78:9 gives a sad commentary concerning the tribe of Ephraim: "The children of Ephraim, being armed and carrying bows, turned back in the day of battle." In other words, in the heat of the battle—when they were most needed—these soldiers withdrew. What a time to desert! *Quititis* (the quitting disease) had apparently infected the whole tribe of Ephraim.

We also live in a "day of battle," a war zone. We are on a battlefield. Christianity is not a pleasure cruise on a luxury liner; it is active duty on a battleship.

How do you handle the stress of the conflict? Do you stand fast and fight, or do you retreat as did the Ephraimites? Our society has raised a generation of quitters rather than stickers. Flight is preferred over fight. It's tragic that quitting has become acceptable. In fact, in certain circles, it's the "in thing." When the heat rises and the going gets tough, many withdraw or bail out altogether. Understand this: Quitting solves nothing! It only postpones a confrontation with reality.

Quititis has infected every segment of society—church, home, school, and work. It is not easily detected. Outwardly, the Ephraimites were highly polished, as smooth as a muscular Marine drill team. But underneath the dress blues were yellow bellies. In fact, the original reads, "they turned back again and again"—not just once, but many times. The Ephraimites were perpetual quitters, making a practice of giving up and never facing the enemy.

Take a look at your track record. Has quitting become habitual with you? Are you prone to look for escape routes when the pressure increases? Abandon your escape mentality. Square your shoulders, soldier, and face the battle head-on!

Quititis usually doesn't manifest itself until pressure is applied. When faced with increased demands, marital disputes, tough subjects, or a cut in pay, many people crack. We, like the Ephraimites, possess the outward equipment but lack inward character and persevering strength. God is not impressed by our performance at rehearsal, such as Sunday morning worship. The real test is when we're on the battlefield. It's there that we prove whether or not we possess perseverance.

If you rely strictly on talent, intellect, and human resources, you will fail miserably. Only inner strength and persevering power can keep you on the battlefield and prevent defeat. Also remember that constant quitting can develop into the habit of quitting. Don't let quitting become a habit.

Again and again in Revelation 2–3, we hear Jesus declare, "He that overcomes..." shall attain something. In other words, he that perseveres and prevails shall receive. Rewards come to the stickers and the finishers! Runs are not scored by reaching third base, nor are touchdowns gained by reaching the five yard line. We can't just compete; we must complete the course.

Races are not always won by the swift but often by those who continue to run and refuse to quit. Christianity is not a sprint but a marathon, which is why perseverance is more important than talent or speed. Perseverance is the only thing that will keep a runner going. And without it, you will never be able to endure disappointments, peer pressure, trials, or adversity.

The genuineness of Christianity is best demonstrated by our willingness to persevere through the struggles of life. No matter what failures, mistakes, and stumbles you make, never stay down. Get back up, and continue to run, "For though a righteous man falls seven times, he rises again... (Prov. 24:16 NIV).

Winston Churchill, speaking at the commencement ceremony of his Alma Mater, condensed his speech into one short powerful phrase: "Never give up! Never give up! Never, never, never give up!"

God wants us to wake up, speak up, pray up, pay up, and look up, but never give up, let up, or back up until the race is done and the victory is won. The only thing worse than quitting is never starting to run. Christians who start but do not finish the race disgrace the Church and discredit Christianity. If God has called you to something, then hang tough and don't quit because nobody can do your assigned job better than you.

Blessed is the man who perseveres under trial, because when he has stood the test, he will receive the crown of life that God has promised to those who love Him (James 1:12 NIV).

The tiny, fragile hummingbird (less than 4 inches long) flies an estimated 500 miles non-stop over the Gulf of Mexico during its migration. That's perseverance! If the tiny hummingbird refuses to quit before he reaches his destination, why should you?

Don't allow discouragement to destroy you, and don't give in to the "I'm tired and depressed, and everyone else is quitting" attitude. My favorite poem reads:

> *No one is beaten 'til he quits.*
> *No one is through 'til he stops.*
> *No matter how hard failure hits.*
> *No matter how often he drops.*
> *A fellow is not down 'til he lies*
> *In the dust and refuses to rise.*
>
> *Fate may bang him around*
> *And batter him 'til he is sore,*
> *But it is never said that he's down*
> *While he bobs up serenely for more.*
> *A fellow is not dead 'til he dies.*
> *Nor done 'til he no longer tries.*[1]

As you encounter deadlines, added expenses, family demands, cutting criticism, and stiff opposition, remember that—rather than correcting your circumstances—quitting just compounds and complicates the matter. Face the adversity head on. Stand strong and fight the good fight.

---

1. Author unknown.

10

Producing Perseverance

A diamond is a lump of coal that just didn't quit!

It's no secret that most of us are not born with great persevering ability. We're actually more prone to quitting than
sticking. Perseverance isn't a given; it's something that has
to be birthed and developed. It's a process that takes time—
a lot of time, sometimes even a lifetime. If you're reading
this book, you're probably well into this process.

How God Builds Perseverance Into a Believer

Because God has called each of us into this arena of
faith, and because perseverance is what we need to finish
the race, God is personally committed to producing this vital ingredient in each one of us. Before this can happen, we
must be willing to submit to the process, however painful it
must be.

1. God permits suffering

According to Romans 5:3-4 (NIV), "...we also rejoice in
our sufferings, because we know that suffering produces
perseverance; perseverance, character; and character,
hope." James 1:3 (NIV) confirms, "...the testing of your
faith develops perseverance."

Real perseverance (and, consequently, character) is produced only during tough times, which might explain why God often permits hurt and hardship to touch the lives of His children. He knows that only tests and trials can produce persevering power and Christ-like character within us. When your heart is breaking and you feel like you're losing your grip, remember that a loving heavenly Father is carefully monitoring everything that comes your way and that the purpose of your trial is to perfect your character.

You must remember three powerful absolutes during these times of suffering:

- God loves you.

I know that this is hard to believe when you miscarry your first child or your employer hands you a pink slip. Always cling to the fact that God loves you, even when it doesn't seem like He's coming through. You are the very object of His love! He has declared,

> *...Fear not, for I have redeemed you; I have summoned you by name; you are Mine. When you pass through the waters, I will be with you; and when you pass through the rivers, they will not sweep over you.... Since you are precious and honored in My sight, and because I love you...* (Isaiah 43:1-2,4 NIV).

The Scriptures remind us, "For whom the Lord loves He chastens" (Heb. 12:6a).

- God is good.

When God doesn't seem to be coming through for you, it's never because He isn't good. The psalmist David proclaimed, "I would have lost heart, unless I had believed that I would see the goodness of the Lord..." (Ps. 27:13). He then shouted this praise, "How great is Your goodness, which You have stored up for those who fear You..." (Ps. 31:19 NIV).

We have this confidence during times of suffering, "No good thing will He withhold from those who walk uprightly" (Ps. 84:11b). During the simple stress points and the devastating breaking points of your life, you can bank on this truth: God is good, all the time!

• God never makes a mistake.

His ways are always perfect. There is no such thing as a divine miscalculation. God's work is error-free, and His plans are flawless. If you are experiencing doubt and confusion, keep in mind: God has a plan and He has everything under control.

He Maketh No Mistake

My Father's way may twist and turn,
My heart may throb and ache
But in my soul I'm glad to know,
He maketh no mistake.

My cherished plans may go astray,
My hopes may fade away,
But still I'll trust my Lord to lead
For He doth know the way.

Tho' night be dark and it may seem
That day will never break;
I'll pin my faith, my all in Him,
He maketh no mistake.

There's so much now I cannot see,
My eyesight's far too dim;
But come what may, I'll simply trust
and leave it all to Him.[1]

Suffering is a universal reality from which Christians are not exempt. Rather than rant and rave, we rejoice and

---

1. Mary Mason, "He Maketh No Mistake" *Pentecostal Evangel* (1972). Used by permission.

count it all joy because we know that every trial we face further strengthens us for the road ahead. Real perseverance can only be produced by anchoring deep and riding out the storm.

2. *God turns up the heat.*

Heat, like heartache, produces inner strength and stamina. Three young Hebrews were on the verge of destruction when the pagan king Nebuchadnezzar had threatened them with the ultimatum, "Bow or burn!" The Babylonian furnace had been turned up seven times its normal temperature. Where was God? Surely there would be some last-minute intervention. But none seemed to appear.

Read the account for yourself in Daniel 3. God allowed these faithful young men to be thrown into a furnace of intense heat. What in the world was He doing? Perhaps in the scorching heat of a Babylonian furnace, God was at work producing perseverance.

While actively involved in competitive long-distance running, I often chose to train in the heat of the summer afternoon, sometimes when the temperature was peaking out between 90-100 Fahrenheit. During such times, my wife (a registered nurse) always questioned my sanity, and my body often agreed with her. But deep down, I knew that heat training would produce greater stamina. Since most runners choose to train in the cool summer mornings and evenings, race day usually brought me rich dividends because my heat training enabled me to run faster and longer.

Maybe you're feeling the heat. If so, rest assured that God is using it to produce in you the fiber necessary to go the distance. It is so that you can be counted a winner and not a wimp. Don't quit because it's hot. It is in kilns of great heat that clay is fired and fashioned for service. It is in crucibles of fervent fire that the highest grades of steel are tempered. And it is in such heated environments that God will prepare us for effective ministry.

When in furnaces of heartache and hardship, never lose sight of God's eternal purpose. If God has permitted it, you can be sure that it's for your eternal good. "Beloved, do not be amazed and bewildered at the fiery ordeal which is taking place to test your quality, as though something strange (unusual and alien to you and your position) were befalling you" (1 Pet. 4:12 AMP). God has given us this promise as well: "When you walk through the fire, you shall not be burned, nor shall the flame scorch you" (Is. 43:2b).

3. God adds weights to our load.

God often places heavy weights on our shoulders, in order to develop our ability to persevere. In essence, Jesus said, "Follow Me and I'll put a cross upon your back." Most world-class athletes train while wearing weights on their wrists, ankles, and waists. Weights build strength and endurance. These weights come off at race time so the athlete can be completely unfettered as he competes for the prize. No cross, no crown. It's just that simple.

You may be wondering what God is doing, or why the load must be so heavy. Often God is training and toughening you for the course ahead. Those people who seem to be bearing heavier burdens are actually being prepared for a greater task down the road, one that will demand tremendous perseverance. Every test we endure further conditions and prepares us for the next one. Every cross we carry in full submission to God's will not only enlarges and strengthens us, but also develops our ability to bear even greater adversities with indescribable ease.

Regardless of the nature or weight of your cross, it is actively working for your good. Furthermore, you can be sure that Jesus will never place a heavier weight on you than you can bear. (See First Corinthians 10:13.)

How the Believer Increases His Persevering Power

God's work is never totally independent of man; therefore, each of us must be committed to the development of perseverance. Developing perseverance requires an ambitious effort. Second Peter 1:5-6,8 (NIV) exhorts:

> For this very reason, **make every effort** to add to your faith goodness; and to goodness, knowledge; and to knowledge, self-control; and to self-control, **perseverance**.... For if you possess these qualities in increasing measure, they will keep you from being ineffective and unproductive....

Perseverance is a matter of conditioning and preparation. Let me illustrate. When I ran my first marathon in Rochester, New York, I was in great shape for a 5- or 10-mile race, but not for a 26.2-mile endeavor. My longest training run had been 12 miles. Needless to say, by mile 20 of the marathon, "I hit the wall" and began walking. I was unable to persevere because I had not adequately prepared.

Invisible, but very real, the runner's "wall" is the quitting point, the point at which indescribable exhaustion, weakness, and despair set in. At the wall, legs weaken, vision blurs, and the will to go on vanishes. It's here where the temptation to quit is the strongest. This mysterious wall appears suddenly. It looms like a great adversary that seems strategically positioned to beat the runner. It is without question the single most difficult barrier for the runner to overcome. In every marathon, scores of athletes "hit the wall" and never recover. They drop out, never to finish the race. You cannot negotiate with the wall. The bottom line is simple—if you don't beat the wall, it will beat you.

Somewhere along the course, every believer also encounters a wall. It may be a point of great disappointment, severe tragedy, painful affliction, or depression. Every day many believers drop out of the race, never to finish. However, careful evaluation has revealed that prepared athletes can run through the wall—while those who are unprepared become victims. A personal wall can devastate an unprepared believer!

Most spiritual tragedies are the result of a lack of preparation, training, and discipline. We prepare for the test through conditioning and training. Regardless of what your frail flesh says, exercise and rigorous workouts are essential.

A football team scrimmages all week to get ready for Sunday's game. A successful runner trains for months before he runs a marathon. An accomplished musician spends tedious hours in rehearsal before the big concert. The diligent student spends long nights studying before taking an exam. The soldier undergoes weeks of intense basic training before he's fit to fight.

Engaging in daily workouts certainly enhances one's ability to endure, succeed, and win. We cannot say enough about the importance of preparation. No success can be attained apart from proper conditioning.

The Bible strongly urges us to engage in such preparatory training: "...Train yourself toward godliness (piety), [keeping yourself spiritually fit]. For physical training is of some value (useful for a little), but godliness (spiritual training) is useful and of value in everything and in every way..." (1 Tim. 4:7-8 AMP). To increase our ability to persevere, we must daily train in prayer and in God's Word.

There is no substitute for prayer preparation. Through prayer, the believer is prepared to face any giant, problem, sickness, or hardship without going down to defeat. A Christian is only as strong as his prayer life. Most believers are weak in perseverance because they are weak in prayer. Prayer always produces persevering power! When the great Charles Spurgeon was asked the secret of his spiritual power he responded, "Knee work! Knee work!" Real persevering power is key to real prayer.

Equally important in preparation is the Word of God. The believer is no match for his wall without the Word! We must read, study, meditate upon, and memorize Scripture to maintain a state of spiritual fitness and readiness. The prophet Isaiah informs us, "But those who wait on the Lord

[in prayer and in His Word] shall renew their strength...
they shall run and not be weary, they shall walk and not faint"
(Is. 40:31). Many believers are spiritually sick—malnourished
from a deficiency of the Word. Discipline yourself to pray
and study. Prove yourself to be a workman who doesn't
need to be ashamed (see 2 Tim. 2:15). Your spiritual life depends on it.

When you encounter your greatest test—perhaps the
death of a loved one, a miscarriage, unemployment, terminal illness, rebellious children—you must be prepared. The
unexpected always devastates the unprepared. Blessed is
the man who is prepared and well-trained in prayer and the
Scriptures so that he can beat the wall of discouragement
and finish his course.

Conditioning involves discipline. Paul the apostle said,
"But [like a boxer], I buffet my body [handle it roughly, discipline it by hardships] and subdue it" (1 Cor. 9:27a AMP).
Discipline means bringing yourself into a state of order and
obedience through training and control. Discipline is what
separates champions from competitors, professionals from
amateurs and athletes from weekend jocks. Be tough on
yourself, because no one else will. Like a runner or a boxer,
push yourself! Gold-medal winners push themselves to their
limits as they train for the Olympic games.

Repeatedly, Jesus called for disciples, not just followers.
A disciple is a disciplined person, one whose life is governed by discipline. The word *disciple* is mentioned (in some
form) 269 times in the New Testament. Strangely enough,
the word *Christian* is used only three times. It seems clear
that we are called to become disciples, not just Christians,
and also we are called to "make disciples" and not just
Christians. (See Matthew 28:19.) Only the person governed
by godly discipline is truly a disciple.

Discipline yourself to pray, study, and persevere. You learn
to persevere by persevering. Sure you've been roughed up a
bit, who hasn't? Maybe recent criticisms have body-slammed

you to the mat. Instead of laying down, you need to get up and move on. Persisting on in the face of failure or disaster produces perseverance. By quitting, you only learn to quit. Break this habit by not giving in to defeat.

Is the course easy? Of course not! Will discouragement ever come? Absolutely! There will always be difficult tasks, dry deserts, bad marriages, stressful home situations, tough subjects, and boring conversation, all of which require perseverance.

Submit to the trials, the heat, and the cross that God permits. Train yourself well in prayer and in the Word of God, and there will always be sufficient stamina to persevere through every quitting point.

11

Endurance:
Passive Perseverance

Trees with deep roots can endure the strongest winds.

So far we have examined *active perseverance*—pressing in, praying through, taking hold. Active perseverance is the strength that a locomotive displays when pulling a heavy train across a bridge, or the power the wind manifests when it sways a mighty oak. It's the power to keep going.

Passive perseverance—endurance—is the strength of the bridge to hold up under the weight of the train, or the power of the mighty oak to withstand the wind's force. Passive perseverance is the power to stand firm and bear the heavy weight of life's difficulties without grumbling.

We read in Hebrews 12:2 that Christ "endured the cross." Verse 3 declares that He also "endured" the bitter hostility of sinners. The Greek word translated "endure" is *hupomeno*. *Hupo* means "under" and *meno* means to stay or endure, hence the literal meaning, "to stay or to hold up under" or "to withstand." The image is that of a beast of burden (an ox or mule) that holds up under the extreme weight of a heavy load.

Some things in life must be endured, rather than conquered or defeated. For example, Christ could not defeat or conquer the cross per se. He simply had to endure it. Likewise, some sicknesses, marriages, difficult circumstances, and tough subjects can only be endured. The trial you are experiencing could be the work of satan, and it could be equally born of the will of God. If it's according to God's sovereign will, then all you can do is submit to the trial and silently endure.

The cross was certainly the work of wicked men who were inspired by satan, but no one would argue that it was also the will of God. For that reason, Jesus submitted to the cross and endured it even though He knew that satan was behind it. Jesus had been beaten beyond recognition and then crucified. "...His appearance was so disfigured...and his form marred beyond human likeness" (Is. 52:14 NIV). What indescribable treatment! "He was oppressed and He was afflicted, yet He opened not His mouth; He was led as a lamb to the slaughter..." (Is. 53:7). Despite the horrible punishment that He was dealt, Christ remained calm and silently endured.

This kind of passive perseverance is rare today, but oh how it preaches! When the centurion that crucified Christ saw His conduct during suffering, he became a believer and declared, "Truly this Man was the Son of God!" (See Mark 15:34.) The centurion never heard Jesus preach but was instead convinced by His ability to endure. He had seen many crucifixions and had heard the cursings and accusations of many a victim. He knew the disastrous toll that the cross took on a man, often bringing the worst out of its victims. Hatred, anger, and bitterness regularly spewed from those crosses. But Christ silently endured, and from His cross flowed love, mercy, and forgiveness. This Man actually forgave the butchers who crucified Him. So powerful was this display of triumphant endurance that it made a believer out of a calloused Roman soldier.

How are you reacting and responding to your cross around other people? Do you blame, complain, pout, and protest? You bring disgrace to Christ and discredit to His Church when you fail to hold up silently under the weight of your circumstances. Our actions and reactions during our times of suffering either draw people closer to Christ or drive them further away.

Trials also reveal a person's inner character. Personal attributes and attitudes always seem to surface when the going gets rough. Those who are uncommitted don't suffer well. Phonies can't endure silently.

Moses was one who endured. According to Hebrews 11:27, "By faith...he endured as seeing Him who is invisible." Moses endured the rejection of his own people, 40 long years of desert exile and the stiff opposition of Pharaoh. Somehow faith in God produces the ability to silently tolerate abuse, opposition, criticism, and mistreatment. Like Moses, we must prove that we can "endure afflictions" before we can qualify for leadership.

The Scriptures command us to "endure hardship" in the following ways:

- As a soldier (2 Tim. 2:3-4).

A soldier is a man engaged in warfare, one who has left civilian life for the rigors of military service. His only consideration is to serve his commanding officers and his country. To do this, he willingly endures the hardships of basic training, stringent rules, and tough military combat. Each believer must "...endure hardship as a good soldier of Jesus Christ" (2 Tim. 2:3).

- As an athlete (2 Tim. 2:5).

An athlete competes for the prize according to a strict set of rules. He must concentrate all of his energy on winning. Ardently focused, the athlete refuses to be sidetracked. The arena in which he competes involves suffering, striving, and stiff resistance, but the athlete endures so that he might be crowned the champion.

- As a farmer (2 Tim. 2:6).

No one exercises more endurance than the farmer. Progressing from seed time to harvest time is no picnic. The farmer must endure indifferent weather conditions, long hours of constant toil, and many mechanical setbacks in order to raise his crops.

We are encouraged by God's Word. "Blessed is the man who endures temptation; for when he has been approved, he will receive the crown of life..." (Jas. 1:12). Later, James says, "Indeed we count them blessed who endure" (Jas. 5:11a). James cites Job as one who championed the art of passive perseverance. In a short period of time, Job lost everything: livestock, children, and health. What a tragic ordeal! However, Job endured. An unsupportive wife, faithless friends, and a year of bitter heartache and physical pain could not derail his faith in God. He withstood the bitter loss and maintained his integrity. What a magnificent exhibition of endurance! Is it any wonder God turned his captivity and restored to him double what he had lost? (See Job 42.)

Bridges are built to endure, or passively withstand, the weight of trains, trucks, cars, and buses. A bridge is built to hold up under tremendous pressure. Christians are also built to endure. Pressure is real. Circumstantial weights can be crushing. Whatever you do, don't collapse. Don't cave in under the pressure: "Be steadfast, immovable" (1 Cor. 15:58). Remember, "He who endures to the end shall be saved" (Mt. 24:13)!

12

Factors That Promote Quitting

Perseverance is just hanging in there in spite of it all.

Many times, quitting appears unavoidable because of certain factors within us or about us.

Weights

Some of you are trying to run in the arena of faith while you're weighed down. You feel like quitting because you can't seem to keep up. Four hundred-pound people don't win races. They can lumber along, but that's about it. For that reason, God gives us this command: "Lay aside every weight...and...run...the race..." (Heb. 12:1b)! You can run with weights, but you can't win!

If you're struggling and are unable to make any significant progress, you may very well have a "weight problem." Anything that holds you back or slows you down is a weight. Attitudes, habits, fears, traditions, stubbornness, fleshly lusts, unforgiveness, bitterness, and prejudice are all weights. Extra baggage is a negative.

The scriptural command calls for aggressive action. In the Amplified Bible, Hebrews 12:1 says, "...Let us strip off

and throw aside every encumbrance (unnecessary weight)...."
Aggressively and determinedly strip off anything that impedes
your spiritual progress!

The ancient Greeks participating in the games wore
weights during race training to help build stamina, as do
modern athletes. When race time came, the weights came
off. Why? Because weights are deterrents to successful running and winning. Weights keep us from reaching our full
potential, hindering victory and limiting progress. We can
run with weights, but we cannot win!

Frank Shorter won the 1972 Olympic marathon. He
credited the victory to the fact that he ran without socks.
Prior to the race, he calculated the weight of a pair of socks
and then multiplied that by the number of strides he would
take over the 26.2 mile course. Although a pair of socks
weighs only a few ounces, the accumulated weight over the
long run could have been devastating. Clearly, one seem-
ingly insignificant weight can cost you victory and success.
When the New International Version of the Bible translates
Hebrews 12:1 as, "throw off everything that hinders," it
means everything.

As you run this race, deal severely with excessive
weights. We are not called to merely run. Anyone can run.
We are called to finish and to obtain the prize (see 1 Cor.
9:24). Don't be content to merely compete. Break from the
pack, strip off the weights, and be a champion!

Sin

The single greatest deterrent to success and progress is
sin. Hebrews 12:1 calls for us to exercise the same aggressive authority when dealing with sin as we do with weights:
"Let us throw off everything that hinders and the sin that so
easily entangles us..." (Heb. 12:1b NIV).

The author of Hebrews has one particular sin in mind,
otherwise he would not have used the singular "sin." There
was one sin he was most concerned about. There is one sin

to which each of us are most vulnerable. We must deal more aggressively with that particular sin than with others. Translators of the New International Version of the Bible use the word *entangle* because it best conveys the meaning from the original Greek text: Sin is like a giant octopus that wraps its tentacles around us and strangles from us every ounce of life, enthusiasm, vitality, faith, and optimism. Some of you feel like quitting simply because a sin you have tolerated is now stifling and short-circuiting God's work in your life. Sin will choke out your desire for God, family, church, and victory.

Unlike weights, sin is not just detrimental; it is deadly. Weights will deter you, but sin will destroy you. You cannot passively deal with sin. You must actively, aggressively, and severely deal with every sin!

Distractions

Distractions, like weights and sins, can deter our progress and set us back spiritually. The author in Hebrews 12:2 (NIV) warns us against such carnal distractions by calling us to "...fix our eyes on Jesus, the author and perfecter of our faith...."

To avoid quitting, Christians must maintain proper perspective. Persevering power is the result of proper perspective. Without a definite focus, one's most ambitious effort becomes meaningless. Hebrews 12:2 challenges us to deliberately look away from everything that has the ability and the power to distract us and divert our focus away from Jesus.

There are four things from which we must "look away" in order to finish.

- Other people.

When you spend too much time examining other people, you can easily become negative and critical of their imperfections. People fail, but Jesus never fails! People disappoint, but Jesus never disappoints! People criticize and condemn, but Jesus says, "Neither do I condemn you" (see

Jn. 8:11). People hurt, but Jesus comforts and cures. People discourage, but Jesus encourages.

- Your situation.

If you focus only on your personal trials and tragedies, you'll become discouraged and absorbed with self-pity. It's so easy to give up when you consider how bad your life may seem. Instead of focusing on your own pain and problems, look to Jesus, who is the prince of peace.

- Worldly attractions.

Worldly attractions can easily become distractions. Nothing distracts a believer any more than the sights and sounds of the world—money, music systems, exquisite houses, expensive clothes. If we're running after the world and its goods, we can't be running after Jesus.

- Yourself.

Self-focus can be disastrous. When we look too long at ourselves, we often see an inferior, inadequate, and incapable person. Self-focused people rarely succeed.

You can't, but Jesus can. You won't, but Jesus will. You're untalented, but Jesus is multi-talented. You're inadequate, but Jesus is adequate. Look away from yourself and look to Jesus instead.

Blondin, the great French tight-rope artist, supposedly erected a star and then focused on it while tight-roping across Niagara Falls back in the late 1890's. He looked away from the people behind him and away from the precarious situation he was in. (*No* situation could be worse than balancing on a one-inch tightrope 600 feet about the turbulent Niagara River.) He looked away from the distracting roar of the falls and away from his own weaknesses and inabilities. Blondin riveted his focus upon a star, and as a result, he was able to do what no man had ever done before: tightrope across Niagara Falls.

Life is like a tightrope. To maintain your balance and walk successfully requires the utmost focus and concentration. Any loss of concentration can cause a mishap or a disastrous fall. Rivet your eyes upon the Morning Star. Concentrate solely on Him, and you'll be amazed at how your difficulties are no longer impossibilities.

As another example, the North Star remains in the same place, unchanging and always dependable. For that reason alone, navigators and mariners use the North Star as their anchor point when charting their courses. They wisely establish a vertical (rather than horizontal) point of reference for direction on the unpredictable seas.

Christ is the Day Star risen in our hearts, always unchangeable and always dependable (see 2 Pet. 1:19 KJV). Abandon the failing, ever-changing horizontal points of reference in your life and instead establish one vertical focus: Jesus Christ.

According to Hebrews 11:27, Moses "...endured as seeing Him who is invisible." In other words, Moses' attention was riveted on the eternal God. He could endure his people's rejection, 40 years of sheep tending in the desert, and the Pharaoh's stiff opposition because his heart was always fixed on God. Moses never flinched. He held on to the vision with a vise-like grip. If you lose sight of who God is, you are finished, for only one who sees the invisible can do the impossible!

To avoid quitting, we need to discipline ourselves (like Blondin and Moses) to look away from everything that is earthly and fallible and look unto Him who cannot fail. Jesus Christ is our undefeated, unfailing, matchless Morning Star and miracle-working Champion. Rivet your eyes, your mind, and your heart on Him. As the psalmist David declared, "My eyes are ever toward the Lord" (Ps. 25:15a).

My wife has coined the phrase "fight to focus" and instills it in our children as she home schools them. A traveling ministry like ours contains many distractions, and our children would be academic failures if they could not maintain proper focus while walking the tightrope over the turbulent waters of travel and church life.

Blondin had to fight to stay focused, and so will you. Focusing on Jesus will be a struggle every step of the way, so fight the good fight and lay hold to eternal life.

Weariness and Fatigue

Weariness is a definite deterrent to progress and success. Nothing has the ability to slow us or abruptly stop us like fatigue. Most of our lives are spent racing back and forth in the fast lane with little time left for meaningful rest or relaxation. We have become the most over-extended, over-committed generation in all of history. Most people can't handle the pace or the pressures of the race. Is it any wonder that people break down and quit so often? Failure often results during times of fatigue.

We've examined the principle of focus in Hebrews 12:2a (NIV): "Let us fix our eyes on Jesus." Now let's examine the following verse: "Consider Him [Jesus] who endured...so that you will not grow weary and lose heart" (Heb. 12:3 NIV). To avoid weariness, you must do more than simply focus on Jesus: You must also consider Him.

To *consider* means "to study and analyze." According to this text, then, we should analyze the courage and endurance Christ displayed while suffering at the hands of evil men. He not only endured grievous opposition and bitter hostility from His peers, but the cruel crucifixion of the cross as well. By studying Him, according to the text, we can avoid growing weary and losing heart.

Christ's race was a grueling ordeal of heartbreak and hardship, but His perseverance enabled Him to not only finish but also perfect the race. Studying Christ's example has a way of renewing both our strength and perspective. If Jesus could endure the cross, surely we can endure our moments of light affliction. There is nothing that we could suffer that Christ Himself hasn't both suffered and triumphed through.

Take some time right now to pinpoint and then renounce—in Jesus' name—any impeding weights or controlling sins in your life. Renounce anything that could keep you from running your race to the fullest. Now take a moment to refocus. Rivet your complete attention and affection upon Jesus. Begin to love Him and study His life as an example of how you can live your own. The fruit of this exercise will be evident for all to see.

13

The Biblical Strategy for Success

A winner is just a loser who won't concede defeat. And a loser is just a winner who refuses to compete.

In the 1960 Olympic games in Rome, Italy, Wilma Rudolph won both the 100-meter and 200-meter dashes. She also ran the anchor leg on the winning 400-meter relay team. She captured all three events in world-record times. How does a child afflicted with polio, scarlet fever, and double pneumonia—someone who had lost the use of one leg—grow up to be the fastest woman in the world?

Wilma Rudolph was born in Tennessee, one of 22 children. She was forced to wear leg braces at age six due to the effects of scarlet fever. As a child, she dared to believe that God could restore her legs. With the help of her brothers and sisters, she persistently practiced walking without her braces. On her twelfth birthday, she surprised everyone by taking off the braces and walking without assistance around the doctor's office. From that day on, she never wore braces again.

Wilma went on to become a star basketball player in high school. While playing in the state basketball championship, one of the referees encouraged her to try running. After basketball season, she went out for track. Wilma immediately began winning races, and by age 16 she was already one of the best runners in the country. She made the Olympic team in 1956 and went on to win a bronze medal in Australia. Unsatisfied with her accomplishment, she diligently trained four more years before winning the three gold medals in Rome in 1960.

Time after time during her youth, Wilma encountered the quitting point. Each time, however, she pressed on with tremendous courage, determination, and faith in God.

Maybe you've been set back physically or financially. Don't give up! Any challenge can be met and every obstacle overcome as you begin to incorporate biblical principles into your life.

Facing tremendous adversity from a prison cell, the apostle Paul penned a strategy that can be used at any quitting point: "I have just one game plan, one strategy that I incorporate, one thing that I do..." (see Phil. 3:12-14).

I've discovered that there are many things that you simply won't have time for if you want to win at life, experience revival, or be successful. Maybe you're stressed out because you have too many irons in the fire and too many pots on the stove. You may be over-extended and over-committed because you're attempting to do all things and be all things to all people. Bill Cosby once said, "I can't give you the formula for success. I can, however, give you the formula for failure—say 'yes' to everyone."

The best solution is to establish a few basic priorities and then devote yourself to them. Priorities are important things, necessary things. Jesus informed Martha, Mary's stressed-out, "workaholic" sister, "But one thing is needed [or necessary]..." (Lk. 10:42). My district superintendent used to counsel the preachers he oversaw with the words, "Don't get caught up in the thick of thin things." What advice! Thin things are unimportant things, insignificant things. Maybe it's time for you to cut back to just a few necessities. Why not start now? The sooner the better.

Paul said, "I discipline my mind to forget those things which are behind" (see Phil. 3:13). What things was Paul referring to? He was referring to sinful lusts and habits, mistakes and failures, hurts and heartaches, all the blown opportunities and bitter experiences of his past.

If you've confessed to and repented of your sins, then they've been forgiven. They are under Christ's blood. God has cast all of your sins into the sea of His forgetfulness, never to be remembered again (see Mic. 7:19). In fact, He has posted a "No Fishing" sign in this sea. The worst possible mistake you could make is to go into that sea with your spiritual rod and reel and try to fish out your ugly past.

What's in the past is past! What has been forgiven by God is no longer a threat to you. There is absolutely no need to fear! People who spend all their time dwelling on the past become miserable and defeated. Don't let the failures of yesterday keep you from the successes of today. What God forgives, He forgets! Ask God to sanctify your "forgetter" so that you can do the same.

Paul also said, "I reach forward to those things which are ahead" (see Phil 3:13b). Have you ever watched the beautiful rhythm of a world-class sprinter? Both arms and legs move with the precision and rhythm of pistons. The very stride of the runner—back and forth, back and forth—speaks of forgetting and reaching. With every stride the runner forgets the mistakes and failures of yesterday and reaches forward to the opportunities and challenges of today. Each step is a step forward, not a step back. What a picture!

To *reach* means to "stretch or extend" yourself. Paul was specific when he said, "I reach forward." Many counselors and mental therapists encourage their clients to reach backward—into the past. This can be a dangerous mistake resulting in more trauma, fear, and depression. Victory comes from reaching forward, not backward!

A familiar Gospel story depicts a woman with an incurable blood disease who reached and stretched to touch the hem of Jesus' garment (see Mk. 5:25-34). This woman had sought for a cure. In fact, she had spent all of her money on physicians. But her condition had only worsened. One day she heard about Jesus. After all, who hadn't? He was the talk of the town. She felt deeply convinced that if she could but touch the hem of His garment, she could be made well.

A large crowd was following Jesus that day. Even for a strong person, it would have been a challenge to get through the mass of people, let alone someone weak with infirmity. This poor infirmed woman was no doubt pushed, kicked, and verbally reprimanded for trying to work her way through the crowd, but she continued to inch her way forward, for she thought, "If I can but touch the hem of His garment, I'll be made well."

It's easy to believe that she was at one point knocked to the ground, perhaps even forced to crawl in order to get through all the people. She could have been kicked and stepped on repeatedly, but one thing is for certain: She never gave up trying to reach the man named Jesus. Her one thought was still, "If I can but touch the hem of His garment, I'll be made well."

Finally she broke through into the small circle where Jesus was teaching—unnoticed by Him because she was behind Him. A few protests could be heard from the crowd, but she continued forward until—devastated by weakness and racked with pain—she could move no further. She mustered enough strength to extend her hand upward. She reached until, finally, the tip of her finger touched the very hem of the Master's garment. Suddenly she felt a surge of power rush through her body. In that moment, the woman knew that she had been made whole!

This persistent warrior could not be denied her victory! She had stretched and strained her sick body, pushing herself to her very limit, until she finally touched the hem of Jesus' robe and was healed. Jesus always reaches for a reacher! To receive from God (or to achieve anything in life) requires an aggressive, determined, forward reach. No one can do your reaching for you.

Olympic champions don't just roll out of bed one morning and say, "Hey, I think I'll go for the gold today." What a joke! No, they engage in years of intense training. Day after day, they push and press, stretch and strain. They refuse to quit no matter how exhausted they feel.

Excellence in any field—music, marriage, ministry, parenting, or preaching—requires much training and straining. To excel, you must press, pray, and practice whether you feel like it or not. It's impossible to excel, improve, or win if you live according to your fickle feelings. The great Green Bay Packer coach, Vince Lombardi, said it best: "There is no gain without pain!" No guts, no glory! Success is sweet, but its secret is sweat.

Paul emphasized, "I reach forward to those things." What things? Those things that are ahead—opportunities and challenges, dreams and goals, adventures and new horizons! Are you reaching forward to those things? Or are you still dwelling on the mistakes and failures of your past?

There is always a risk in reaching. When you choose to reach forward toward new challenges and adventures, you run the risk of disappointment and criticism. When you choose to reach toward people, you run the risk of rejection and hurt. And when you reach upward to lay hold to lofty dreams and goals, there is always the danger of failure and defeat. Whenever we go for something that is beyond our present grasp, there is always risk involved. Within each of us something is born that says, "Reach! Pull out the stops and go for it!" If you suppress that drive you'll begin to stagnate, emotionally and spiritually. If you stifle that inner drive to reach, you're finished! For, in the day you stop reaching, you stop living! Don't ever be content with that which is within your grasp. Dare to extend yourself! Put forth an ambitious effort and lay hold of your dream.

A great painter was once asked, "Of all your great works of art, which one do you consider your greatest?" The artist responded, "My next one." He was always reaching forward to a higher level of success and excellence.

On the tomb of an Alpine guide is the inscription, "He died climbing." In other words, he died reaching up toward new heights. What a way to go!

As Paul said, "This one thing I do! This is my strategy for success and victory! I discipline my mind to forget! And I reach…!" (See Philippians 3:13.)

The final point in Paul's strategy for success was "I press toward the goal" (verse 14). To *press* means to "go forward with an ambitious, determined effort." The word speaks of movement, not just motion.

The word *press* also indicates resistance. As you strive to excel, you will always meet resistance. In this Christian race, our every move will be contested by the enemy. For every advance there will be an attack. To win we must press through every resistance.

Christianity is not a "go with the flow," path of least resistance, lifestyle. In this arena, the wind is not always at your back. In fact, sometimes we're called to run headlong into the strong winds of resistance. Wilma Rudolph pressed through the physical and emotional resistance in her life to become a world champion. Sadly, many people quit at the first sign of resistance.

Taking the path of least resistance can often spell doom. Two young Africans were once paddling their canoe down the peaceful blue waters of the Zambaze River. Little did they know that beneath those peaceful waters was a large crocodile. Suddenly the crocodile surfaced and with one quick accurate lunge he grabbed for one of the boys. As he made his lunge, the canoe tipped over. Both Africans fell into the water, panic-stricken. One boy remembered the advice of an old tribal leader: If you are ever in crocodile-infested waters, you should swim upstream because the crocodile always swims downstream to find his prey. This he did, and after several anxious moments of strenuous swimming, he safely reached the shore.

The other boy watched his friend swim upstream, fighting the strong current. He decided to swim downstream in order to get to shore faster and easier. He was doing just fine, going with the flow. But just as he got to shore and lifted one leg from the water, something grabbed his other leg and pulled him back into the river. That was the last anybody ever saw of that boy. Apparently the blood-thirsty crocodile had been following him all the way downstream.

Downstream is dangerous. Christians are not called to take the path of least resistance. We are called to fight the current, reach forward, and press toward the mark!

Tom Dolan won a gold medal in the 400-meter individual medley at the 1996 Olympic games in Atlanta, Georgia. The gold came at a high price, however. Dolan had developed exercise-induced asthma. His windpipe was 20 percent smaller than normal, making it even harder for him to breathe air into his lungs.

While training for the Olympics, Dolan put himself through a grueling training program that included swimming more than 12 miles a day, plus lifting weights. His single-minded persistence kept him in the pool six hours a day, seven days a week—all for one four-minute race.

While engaging in these strenuous workouts, Dolan would occasionally pass out from the asthma. On at least two occasions, he was taken to the emergency room. But despite physical adversity, he continued to press on, refusing to be limited by his physical problems. Tom Dolan couldn't always breathe, but he sure could swim!

Paul said, "I press toward the goal." Do you have a goal that you're pressing toward? What are your dreams and ambitions? Victor Frankl, a Viennese psychiatrist who spent years in the concentration camp at Auschwitz during World War II, declared, "Not having a goal is more feared than not reaching a goal. I would rather attempt to do something great and fail than attempt to do nothing and succeed."

Life's greatest tragedy does not lie in not reaching a goal, but in not having a goal to reach. Establish some spiritual goals, or some numerical goals for your church, some marriage goals, family goals, educational goals, or career goals.

Seek to excel and improve. Give yourself something to reach for; make sure that your reach exceeds your grasp; and never let adversity or resistance keep you from attaining your goal. Some days, it might seem like for every step forward you take two back. Setbacks are real, but for the child of God they are only temporary. Our call is not to retreat but to advance and to press on. It isn't a disgrace to die with goals unreached, but it is a disgrace not to reach.

"I press toward the goal for the prize..." (Phil. 3:14). Christ is life's ultimate prize. In this very context, Paul said, "What was gain to me I counted loss...that I might win Christ" (see Phil. 3:7-8). There is nothing that you can attain or achieve that can compare to Christ. He is the prize of all prizes, the prize of the high calling!

If you have everything but Christ, you have nothing. But if you have nothing but Christ, you have everything. Life's highest ambition is to win Christ!

Life's true gold is not found in medals, trophies, diplomas, degrees, fame, or fortune, but only in a life-changing relationship with Jesus Christ. What shall it profit a runner, a cyclist, or a swimmer if he or she wins an Olympic event and a gold medal but loses the real race and prize? What shall it profit a man if he gains a temporal prize (e.g., Heisman Trophy, Nobel Peace Prize, Medal of Honor) but loses the eternal prize? (See Matthew 16:26.)

At the finish line, according to First Corinthians 13:12 and First John 3:2, we shall see Jesus face to face. One song-writer understood the significance of this prize when she penned the words,

> *It will be worth it all,*
> > *When we see Jesus.*
> *Life's trials will seem so small*
> > *When we see Christ.*
> *One glimpse of His dear face,*
> > *All sorrow will erase,*
> *So bravely run the race*
> *Til we see Christ.*[1]

The prize is what motivates athletes to persevere. Our motivation is Christ. Games played for something other than Christ are ultimately empty.

What a dynamic strategy Paul employed—forgetting, reaching, and pressing. The biblical challenge is to press on-ward toward the goal for the prize of God's high calling. (God's call upon your life is a high calling.) Tragically, many people settle for the low call—a worldly calling—instead of the high, heavenly calling. These become content with God's permissive will rather than His perfect will. Stop listening for the low calling and tune your ear to God's high call. Rather than listening to the arrogant voices of Holly-wood entertainers or professional athletes, listen for God's still, small voice saying, "This is the way, walk ye in it" (see Is. 30:21 KJV).

Maybe you've been living beneath God's will. Maybe you're only a fraction of the person God intends for you to be. Begin now to press through the clamor and confusion of your life. It's imperative that you hear God's voice, know His heart, and find His perfect will. Settling for anything

---

1. Esther Kerr Rusthoi, "When We See Christ," 1941.

less will be settling for something you don't want, something that will bring you heartache and grief the rest of your life. Strive for the high call and the perfect will of God instead!

Let me encourage those of you who have already answered the high call of God and are presently involved in Christian service. Serving God is no duty or drudgery, but a delight. It's not only a high calling, but a high honor!

Are you beaten down? Press on! Feeling somewhat depressed? Press on! Hurting? Press on! Discouraged? Press on! Hassled by adversaries? Press into the secret hiding place of God's presence. Feeling dry and spiritually thirsty? Press into the river of His Spirit and into the fullness of His love! Experiencing resistance? Press through the criticism, affliction, and pain. Press through to victory!

It was May 13, 1940. France and the rest of Western Europe were under the domination of Hitler. England stood alone and faced almost certain invasion. Winston Churchill stood before the British House of Commons. He was commanding the helm of a fearful and deeply discouraged nation. Nevertheless, he called for England's best, with words that were like steel:

> "I have nothing to offer but blood, toil, tears and sweat. We have before us many, many months of struggle and suffering...You ask, what is our goal? I can answer in one word: It is victory. Victory at all costs: victory in spite of all terror: victory, however long and hard the road may be; for without victory there is no survival."[2]

Real Christianity has never been for the soft or effeminate. Christians have always been called to "blood, toil,

---

2. Winston Churchill, (1874–1965). First speech as prime minister of Great Britain, "Victory at All Costs," *Grolier's Multimedia Encyclopedia*, 1996.

tears and sweat." Victory and revival cost something. But to give up, to quit, to compromise and concede the victory costs so much more! You will lose your courage, your convictions, and your dignity. Surely it will cost you to follow Christ, but overshadowing the cost is the glory of the prize that yet lies ahead! And now we press toward the goal for the prize.

"Victory at all costs: victory in spite of all terror: victory, however long and hard the road may be..."

14

Midnight Wrestling

Desperation is always better than despair!

Jacob encountered God on the banks of the Jabbok (a tributary of the Jordan River) in a midnight wrestling match. It was one long night of soul-searching, heart-rending repentance, and spiritual warfare. For the first time in his life, Jacob had a power encounter with God. This encounter not only transformed Jacob's character, but his name as well.

Although Jacob was the son of Isaac and grandson of the great patriarch Abraham, he had never had a firsthand experience with God. He knew God only as the God of his father and grandfather. He was the younger twin of Esau, grabbing hold of his brother's foot during their birth. Even as an infant, he demonstrated an aggressive personality: He was not to be denied!

As a young man, Jacob longed for the birthright that legally belonged to Esau, the firstborn. In fact, he spent many days and nights dreaming and scheming about ways to deceive his brother into forfeiting the birthright. Jacob knew what he wanted, and with great tenacity he pursued it until he obtained it. Still not satisfied, he proceeded to swindle the corresponding blessing from his brother as well. Jacob's double deception so provoked Esau's anger that Jacob literally had to flee for his life.

After 20 years of separation, Jacob decided to return to his homeland. When Esau heard of Jacob's return, he organized an army of 400 men to ensure revenge. It was Esau's chance to even the score. For the first time in his life, Jacob had his back against the wall. He was between a rock and a hard place with no escape route in sight. His bag of tricks was empty, and he considered himself as good as dead. He desperately needed God. For Jacob, this was the end of the line.

When Jacob got desperate, he got alone. He sent his family on ahead. So often solitude is the key to victory. When you're truly desperate, you don't need counselors, minister, friends, or family—just time alone with God. The clock was ticking, and Esau's troops would arrive in less than 12 hours. Jacob finally had to face himself and deal with his own deceptive nature.

Three people live in each individual: The person he thinks he is, the person others think he is, and the person that God knows he is. Jabbok, where Jacob found himself, represents a place of struggle, where we deal severely with the person that God knows we are. It's a place of emptying or pouring out. It would take all night to empty all the deceit, pride, and self-reliance out of Jacob. Like Jacob, most of us don't get to Jabbok until we're desperate—when the divorce papers are served, the diagnosis is terminal, our finances fail, the church splits, or our car is wrecked.

There, at the water's edge under a moon-lit sky, "A Man wrestled with [Jacob] until the breaking of day [dawn]" (Gen. 32:24b). Some theologians propose the "man" to be an angel. Others see the "man" as an Old Testament appearance of Christ. The text, however, identifies this "man": "You have struggled with God...and have prevailed" (Gen. 32:28b).

In previous chapters, we've examined an aggressive perseverance, one that takes hold and refuses to let go until the answer arrives. Jacob demonstrated this kind of perseverance. He not only wanted divine intervention in regards to his brother Esau, but he also wanted deliverance from his marred character. Surely he meant business that night. When he took hold of his opponent, he cried, "I will not let you go unless you bless me! I'm holding on until a change takes place!"

Jacob was not only wrestling with the Lord, but also with himself. That night he came face to face with the shallow third-generation believer that he was. When asked, "What is your name?" suddenly the painful realization struck. "Jacob," he softly confessed. "Deceiver. Pretender. Schemer. Hypocrite. All of this and more." For the first time, he saw himself as he really was.

The conflict raged all night. Gripped with exhaustion and overcome with fatigue, Jacob wrestled on. He fought through the night, determined to receive God's blessing. In Judges 8:4 we read of Gideon and his band of 300 soldiers in their pursuit of the kings of Midian. The text describes them as being "exhausted but still in pursuit." Exhaustion is not license to quit. Victories are won whenever exhausted soldiers continue to pursue.

Amazingly, Jacob prevailed. The same tenacious grit that could not deny him birth, the birthright, or the blessing of his father Isaac was manifest once again. Though overwhelmed with weakness, Jacob refused to quit. Ultimately, the Lord declared, "You have struggled with God and have prevailed." *Prevail* means to gain control or to win the victory: Jacob had wrestled and prevailed!

Many of you, just like Jacob, need to step into that spiritual arena of prayer. You need to take hold of God and His mighty promises and refuse to let go until God answers.

Wrestling is not an option. It is an obligation. It's a part of our job description. Victory can only be achieved as we take hold of God in prayer and wrestle. Defeat is the result of not wrestling. Today's Church doesn't need any more experts, comedians, specialists, or counselors. What it truly needs in this late hour is more wrestlers—those who can prevail until revival, healing, and deliverance come.

You've fought so long and hard without any apparent progress. You're discouraged by what you see (or don't see). You're at the quitting point. Keep wrestling, keep seeking, keep pressing in until you prevail. We only lose when we give up. Take hold, friend, and don't let go!

15

The Journey
Is Too Great

Trying times are never times to quit trying!

Queen Jezebel was outraged! Ahab had just recapped everything that had recently taken place on Mount Carmel, and she had heard every detail. Elijah had called the bluff of her 850 Baal-worshiping cronies and then rebuilt the altar of the Lord, calling fire down from Heaven and convincing all Israel that the Lord alone was God. After a time of repentance and revival, Elijah ordered the slaughter of all 850 of the queen's prophets.

Jezebel exploded with anger and immediately sent a telegram to Elijah saying, "I'm going to get you, Preacher! Within 24 hours, you'll be dead meat!"

Now Elijah wasn't your easily intimidated type. He was confrontational, bold, and courageous. But on this particular occasion, he panicked. Feeling threatened by Jezebel, Elijah took off. He not only left town, but he headed 95 miles south into the wilderness area of Beersheba. He ran for his life, even dropping off his servant and traveling alone for another full day.

Wearied by the searing heat and strong winds, Elijah finally collapsed under a juniper tree (see 1 Kings 19:4 KJV). Juniper trees (more precisely called "broom bushes") were welcome sights for desert travelers: They were the only shrubs large enough to offer protection from the desert's intense sun and wind.

Curled up beneath this bush, Elijah began to pray, "I've had it! I've had enough! I can't take it anymore! I want out! Please take me home, Lord!" Elijah was desperate and suicidal. Have you ever had such a prayer time? At some point of utter exhaustion, you've cried out, "I've had it! I want out of this marriage, this job, this home life, this school, this church, this ministry!" Maybe you've even thought of suicide.

Ours is a day of letdowns, put-downs, rundowns, and breakdowns. Each of us has been victimized. Possibly you've even cried out in despair, "I can't handle this pressure and stress any longer!"

Some people battle physical affliction and discomfort, and finally decide that enough is enough. Others endure months or years of abuse—mental, emotional, and physical. Some parents tolerate unprecedented disrespect and rebellion from their children. "I can't take it anymore!" they finally confess. Others endure lengthy bouts with loneliness, depression, fatigue, fear, and stubborn sinful habits. "Enough!" is their cry of desperation. Enough hurt! Enough heartache! Enough abuse! Enough confusion! Enough suffering! Enough is enough!

Elijah saw himself as one in a long line of failures. "I'm no better than my fathers. They failed, and now I'm failing. Why should I keep on trying? What's the use?" (See 1 Kings 19:4). Elijah had more than a simple stress point. He had reached the quitting point.

A certain story I heard also emphasizes this: Two preachers went out for a round of golf. They came to a particular hole where each had to hit the ball over a large pond to reach the green. The first preacher stepped up to his ball, squared himself, and took his swing, driving the ball across the pond and within three inches of the hole.

The second preacher was less fortunate. He stepped up to his ball, squared himself, took his best stroke, and— "Plop!" his ball landed right in the middle of the pond. He dropped a second ball, squared himself, took the best stroke he was capable of, and—lo and behold—once again the ball landed right in the middle of the pond. For ball number three, he squared himself, best stroke, and yet again, "Plop!" right in the middle of the pond. A fourth ball suffered the exact same fate. Frustrated by his failure to get the ball across the pond, the preacher threw his golf club into the pond and shouted, "I quit!"

The first preacher said, "Oh, come on, Brother! You can't quit golf."

"I'm not quitting golf," snapped the discouraged preacher. "I'm quitting the ministry!"

Apparently, this preacher felt like a failure as a husband, a dad, a pastor, a teacher, a preacher, and (now) a golfer. Several years of frustration all came to a head on the golf course that day.

Have you ever been overcome with that feeling of failure? After months or years with no results, progress, or growth, sometimes you might wonder what there is to live for. I suspect that's where some of you are right now. This is your quitting point. Many spouses have already quit on their marriages, they just haven't informed their partners. Many pastors have already quit on their churches, they just haven't informed the church boards. Many students have already quit on their studies, they just haven't informed their teachers.

Elijah had reached the quitting point. Totally exhausted and emotionally drained, he fell asleep. Similarly, it's easy to fall asleep to the will and purpose of God during times of discouragement and emotional drain. In fact, most failure occurs during these times.

Elijah, just like many of you, was desperate for a fresh touch from God. In fact, his greatest need was to be touched by God. The story unfolds beautifully in First Kings 19, for God sent an angel to tenderly touch His servant. It's interesting to note that God didn't chasten Elijah or clobber him over the head for sulking and pouting. God didn't reprove him or rebuke him for running away and deserting his post. God didn't say, "Shape up or ship out, you flunky!" Neither did God put him on a guilt-trip by suggesting, "You should have had more faith!"

Don't you just hate it when people lay a guilt trip on you? "If only you had more faith, you wouldn't be driving that old clunker of a car." Or perhaps (and much worse), "If only you had more faith, you wouldn't have that cancer." Be thankful that God isn't in the condemning, guilt-trip business.

Without question, sometimes we need to be scolded, but sometimes we just need to be tenderly touched by God. He longs to touch you, burned-out Sunday school teacher! He longs to touch you, stressed-out mom! He longs to touch you, wearied prayer warrior! He longs to touch you, depressed single adult! Frustrated student, discouraged dad, exhausted pastor: No matter who you are, He longs to touch you!

The Bible assures us that God is "a very present help in trouble" (Ps. 46:1). If you only knew how much God longs to touch you. He is right here right now to touch you. Pause just for a moment and yield to His outstretched hand. At this moment, you have no greater need than to experience a fresh touch from God.

God is so faithful that He not only touches us, but also provides us with the sustenance and nutrition we need to continue on the journey. Did you know that God is in the catering business? As Elijah slept, God spread a table for him in the desert. And this was, by no means, the first time that God had supernaturally provided for Elijah. (See First Kings 17:1-6.)

The angel touched him and said, "Arise and eat." When Elijah opened his eyes, there at his head was a cruse of water and a cake baking on the coals. Can you imagine what a cruse of ice-cold, crystal-clear spring water would mean to a sun-parched desert traveler? Within seconds, Elijah had that cruse to his lips, and he drank until he had completely exhausted the supply. The cruse symbolizes refreshing. When you're at the quitting point—at rock bottom or in the driest of deserts—you become desperate for refreshing!

God promises to refresh us:

The poor and needy seek water, but there is none, their tongues fail for thirst. I...will not forsake them. I will open rivers in desolate heights, and fountains in the midst of the valleys; I will make the wilderness a pool of water, and the dry land springs of water (Isaiah 41:17-18).

Soon after this promise, He also says, "...I will give waters in the wilderness and rivers in the desert, to give drink to My people, My chosen" (Is. 43:20). And again, "For I will pour water on him who is thirsty, and floods on the dry ground; I will pour My Spirit on your descendants..." (Is. 44:3). The Holy Spirit is the cruse of refreshing from which we drink and are refreshed.

Every marathon course (26.2-mile race) is peppered by refreshment tables, and each table contains scores of glasses filled with water and high-energy drinks such as Gatorade. These tables are strategically placed about every two or three miles. Woe be to the runner who passes by without taking time to drink, for he will surely collapse with fatigue and dehydration. The only way to prevail through the marathon's many quitting points is to constantly refuel the muscles by drinking plenty of fluids.

Have you been passing by the many spiritual refreshment stands (Bible studies, prayer meetings, altar services, and revival services) that God has established along the course? If so, you will soon become completely drained and drop out of the race. Friend, it's time to "hit the cruse" and be refreshed!

Peter preached, "Repent...so that times of refreshing may come from the presence of the Lord" (Acts 3:19). The Amplified Bible renders this verse as, "So repent...that times of refreshing (of recovering from the effects of heat, of reviving with fresh air) may come from the presence of the Lord." The Greek word translated "refreshing" is *anapsuxis*, literally meaning "a recovery of breath."

Are you out of breath? Are you winded from the reckless pace of this rat race? You're not alone, my friend. Many are out of breath, panting and desperately gasping for spiritual air. Athletes battle fatigue; many struggle to breathe properly until they get their second wind. Suddenly, breathing becomes easier, oxygen rushes to the muscles, and there comes a surge of fresh strength.

"Times of refreshing," or a second wind, come through repentance. As you deny yourself and humbly renounce the hidden works of unrighteousness in your life, you will begin to experience a second wind, along with a new desire to serve the Lord.

Although we never grow tired *of* the Lord's work, we often grow tired *in* the Lord's work. The work of the ministry can be extremely taxing. Serving God can be both physically and emotionally draining. Therefore, God wants us to seek out resting places, without letting them become quitting places. If you don't periodically find a resting place where you can be refreshed, a quitting place will surely find you. Resting points keep us from quitting points! Jesus called, "Come to Me, all you who labor and are heavy laden, and I will give you rest" (Mt. 11:28).

One of my favorite prayers simply says,

Slow me down, Lord.

Ease the pounding of my heart by the quieting of my mind.

Steady my hurried pace with a vision of the eternal reach of
*   time.*

Give me, amid the confusion of the day,
*   the calmness of the everlasting hills.*

Break the tensions of my nerves and muscles with the sooth
*   ing music*
*   of the singing streams that live in my memory.*

Teach me the art of taking minute vacations—
of slowing down to look at a flower,
to chat with a friend,
to pat a dog,
*   to smile at a child,*
*   to read a few lines from a good book.*

Slow me down, Lord,
*   and inspire me to send my roots deep*
*   into the soil of life's enduring values,*
*   that I may grow toward my greater destiny.*

Remind me each day
*   that the race is not always to the swift;*
*   that there is more to life than increasing its speed.*

Let me look upward to the towering oak and
*   know that it grew great and strong because it grew slowly*
*   and well.*[1]

Anyone involved in full-time Christian service should schedule "break-away" time for both spiritual and physical refreshment at least twice (if not three or four) times a year. You owe this resting time to yourself, your spouse, children, church, and (most importantly) God. Jesus set the example after a demanding evangelistic endeavor, when He called the apostles to, "...Come ye yourselves apart into a deserted

1. Tim Hansel, *When I Relax I Feel Guilty* (David C. Cook Publishing Co., 1979).

place, and rest a while" (Mk. 6:31a KJV). Maybe you've heard it said, "If we don't come 'apart', we'll soon come apart."

In our hectic, success-driven world, we often need to be reminded of the importance of setting aside time for holy rest. Some of you are workaholics, always trying to prove something by overloaded schedules and constant activity. You wear the symptoms of burnout as a medal of honor, confusing activity with blessing. May each of us who are actively involved in Christian service heed the biblical command to "rest in the Lord" (Ps. 37:7)!

I recently saw a bumper sticker which read, "Practice Safe Stress." Stress can be devastating. The only way to practice safe stress is to get sufficient rest and trust completely in the Lord's grace and goodness.

Whereas the cruse symbolizes refreshing, the cake symbolizes nourishment. God knows that to finish the race we need both refreshment and nourishment. God calls each one of us to "Arise and eat!" "Come and dine!" and "Taste and see that the Lord is good!"

God prepares tables of nourishment, not only in deserts, valleys, and wildernesses, but also in war zones. David declared, "You prepare a table before me in the presence of my enemies" (Ps. 23:5a). In order to keep performing, we need to be nourished. Surely the cake that God provided was a "high-carbo cake"—one rich in carbohydrates. Sports nutritionists tell us that carbohydrates continue to burn—thus fueling the muscles—long after all the other foods in the body have been burned up. Marathon runners "carb-up" before the big race, energizing themselves to go the distance.

The Bible is our "high-carbo cake." Jesus said, "Man shall not live by bread alone, but by every word that proceeds from the mouth of God" (Mt. 4:4b). This Bread of Life is the only bread that never grows stale! Job said, "I have treasured the words of His mouth more than my necessary food" (Job 23:12b). The Bible contains all the sustaining nutrients that you need to stay on track and finish the course.

If you're growing spiritually weak, you'd better check your diet. A constant diet of spiritual junk food won't cut it on this journey. Martin Luther once said, "The soul can do without all things except the Word of God." Only by drawing daily from the cruse and the cake can you successfully guard against quitting.

After eating and drinking, Elijah went back to sleep. First Kings 19:7 informs us that "the angel of the Lord came back the second time." Elijah experienced a second visitation. Touched again, he awakened and found another cruse and another cake. He was the recipient of a double touch—a double portion of spiritual refreshment and nourishment! Why the second touch and the second portion? Because, according to verse 7, the angel said, "The journey is too great for you."

God knew that Elijah would not make it far in the strength of one touch and one portion, so He provided him another. Likewise, God knows that you can't make it far in the strength of one prayer meeting or one Bible study. We need multiple times of refreshing if we are going to endure to the end without quitting. One touch is not enough! More infilling and more carbo-loading is required to finish the course.

Without a double portion of the Spirit and the Word, you will surely quit when exhaustion sets in during the late stages of the race. You cannot be equal to the journey apart from a double portion! Your task, trial, job, ministry, temptation, affliction, or indebtedness is simply too great. You're no match, in yourself, for what you're facing. The adverb *too* speaks of being excessive or beyond degree. In effect, God is saying, "There is excessive stress, pressure, hardship, and difficulty involved in what you are facing and fighting."

Elijah went another 40 days—another 130 miles—in the strength of that juniper tree prayer meeting. There is no telling how far a man can go or how much a man can take after he's been on his knees "hitting the cruse and consuming the cake."

Some years ago, during the darkest hours of my life, I realized that I was facing a challenge far too great for me. Night after night I pulled the blankets over my head and prayed to God that I would not have to wake up in the morning. Like Elijah, I was suicidal. I was on my personal version of Heartbreak Hill and at my quitting point. Daily I prayed for a double portion and submitted to the fresh touch of God. I knew full well that I could not make it apart from an abundance of God's Spirit and Word. If God had not touched and refreshed me, I would have surely quit. But His tender, gentle touch enabled me to persevere through the tough times and to experience recovery. You can find that same sustaining power as you face quitting points in your life.

Most believers don't really have a clue as to what the future holds. Only one thing is certain: The journey is too great, the climb is hard, and the battle is intense. Our enemy is tough, the challenge is awesome, the risk is high, and our suffering can be bitter. And our only safeguard against quitting is a double touch and a double portion.

16

Empty Nets

Everything you excel in today began in the deep crevices of some failure.

Pete, Andy, Jim, and John were partners in the fishing business. These men were experienced fishermen—professionals, not weekend enthusiasts. Fishing was their life. They knew all the latest techniques. They wrote the books, and they taught the seminars on "How to Be a Successful Fisherman."

In Luke 5, these four expert, experienced fishermen docked their boats and washed their nets. It looked like they were going to hang up their gear and call it quits. Have you ever felt like docking your own boat and hanging up your nets?

These four fishermen were discouraged, and rightly so. They'd fished all night, and had nothing to show. Nothing is any more frustrating and embarrassing to a fisherman than having empty nets and empty boats. Who could be satisfied with emptiness?

- Nobody likes coming home to an empty house with empty cupboards and to go to sleep in an empty bed.

- Nobody likes having an empty bank account, gas tank, or stomach.

- Nobody likes an empty church with empty class-rooms, pews, and altars.

Emptiness always results in frustration and discouragement—sometimes even embarrassment. On the other hand, fullness is a law of life. Fullness brings satisfaction. Fill a man's stomach, and he'll be easy to live with. Fill a woman's purse, and she'll be easy to live with.

These fishermen were empty and at the quitting point. They felt inadequate and incapable, especially because they were supposed to be experts. They were supposed to know what they were doing.

Can you identify with their situation? Perhaps you're failing at marriage, parenting, teaching, pastoring, language studies, or just managing your finances. Maybe you're an authority in your field—you feel like you should know what you're talking about—but despite your knowledge and experience, you're still failing.

The moment Jesus entered Peter's boat, things began to turn around. If you find yourself overcome with failure, the very best advice I can give you is to get Jesus in your boat as well. Take Him aboard! Partner with the Lord of the seas! Get Jesus involved in your marriage, music, and ministry, in your housework, schoolwork, and homework.

Make Jesus the pilot of the ship. I like the bumper sticker that reads, "If Jesus is your co-pilot, switch seats." Don't make Jesus the co-pilot; instead, let Him steer the ship. Only He can get you around the rocks of destruction.

These four fishermen had already docked their boats and washed their nets. They were through fishing for the day—perhaps for the rest of their lives. But Jesus came onboard, did some teaching, and then ordered them, "Launch out into the deep and let down your nets for a catch" (Lk. 5:4).

Their immediate response was one of reluctance and resistance. "Master," Pete protested, "We have toiled all night and caught nothing... ." Notice that Peter addressed Jesus as "Master"—as someone with authority. Jesus is master of the seas, master of the harvest, master of His Church, and master of every situation! He is the supreme master of the universe!

"Master," Pete objected, "You don't understand what we've just gone through. We've labored all night. We've worked our fingers to the bone. We've put forth every conceivable effort. We're drained! Exhausted!

"And look! We've got nothing to show. Zip. Zero. Nada. Look at our nets, our boats—they're all empty!"

I know you can relate to these feelings of frustration. Your church congregation has knocked on every door in town. You've put on every conceivable program. Maybe you've implemented every idea, tool, and strategy, but nothing has happened. There's no growth, progress, or revival. Pews are still empty.

Maybe you've been to every doctor and every faith healing service. Maybe you've been in every healing line at every prayer meeting, but there has been no improvement in your condition.

Maybe you've been to every marriage counselor and seminar. You've worked hard to save your marriage, but nothing has changed.

Maybe it's dieting that frustrates you. Exercise, pills—you've tried everything, but you have nothing to show for all your effort. Not one pound has been lost.

Perhaps you've been working three jobs, 80 hours per week, desperately trying to get out of debt, but nothing is happening. As soon as you think you can make ends meet, somebody moves the ends. Instead of getting ahead, you keep falling behind.

After working all those years at your church or company, you feel you have nothing to show for your efforts. There's no sign of a raise, promotion, recognition, or appreciation.

After all the time, effort, and love that you gave your kids, they've turned out differently than you've hoped. You can't see any positive sign in their lives.

Maybe, just like these fishermen, you keep casting your nets and coming back with nothing at all. You're trying to win, but you're losing. You're trying to succeed, but you're failing.

The good news is, it's okay to fail. If you're not failing, you're not growing. Sometimes God purposely allows us to fail so that we will trust more completely in Him. I'm convinced that many times when we toil and try, we should be resting and trusting instead. When you try, you fail, but when you trust, you succeed. Stop toiling and trying in your own strength. Trust in God.

Trust in the Lord with all your heart, and lean not on your own understanding; in all your ways acknowledge Him, and He shall direct your paths (Proverbs 3:5-6).

Failure is inevitable. Everyone fails. Just remember that it's better to try and fail than to quit! Remember Thomas Edison? He failed in 700 experiments before he succeeded in creating the light bulb. His refusal to quit finally spelled success. Babe Ruth struck out 1,330 times, but his refusal to quit led to 714 home runs. Winston Churchill once said, "Success is going from failure to failure without the loss of enthusiasm."

Before an artist finishes a masterpiece, he suffers through many mistakes and failures. Before a musician thrills an audience, he spends hours in practice making mistake after mistake.

Let failure be your teacher, not your undertaker. Failure doesn't have to be final! One failure doesn't make you a failure any more than one achievement makes you a success. One broken dream should never bring the end of dreaming.

The Buffalo Bills are my favorite football team. Okay, okay! I know they might have lost four consecutive Super Bowls between 1991 and 1994, but in doing so they proved to all the world that failure doesn't have to be final. They kept coming back, didn't they? They demonstrated resilience—the ability to rebound or spring back quickly. Sure, they might have been down, but they could never be counted out.

The whole country could identify with the Buffalo Bills during this time because everyone has failed at some point. By failing, the Bills truly became America's team! Few people can relate to a success figure, but we all understand the sting of perpetual failure. Those Bills preached a powerful sermon during those years: Despite their failures, they proved that you could bounce back from any situation. All it took was commitment and perseverance.

It's all right to fail, just don't quit. It's all right to slip, just don't let go. Tie a knot and hang on. It's all right to fall, just don't stay down. Never forget, everything you excel in today began in the deep crevices of some failure. I challenge you to view every failure as a delay and not a defeat, as a temporary detour rather than a dead-end street.

Jesus knew that these four fishermen had failed to catch even one fish during a long night of toil. Nonetheless, He said, "Launch out!" So what if the nets are empty! Go back out and don't quit! One failure, however inexcusable, should never become a permanent handicap.

Even the best baseball players experience mid-season slumps and go days without a hit. They swing, but they keep missing the ball. Some have a swinging flaw or timing problem. Still others lack motivation and ambition; they just go through the motions. With their passion gone, it might take weeks before they can recover their dynamics and make a positive contribution to the team. Most coaches won't bench a slumping player: They know that the only way to break out of a slump is to keep stepping up to the plate and swinging away.

I once heard pastor Tony Evans preaching about the "same ol' same ol' disease." You know, we get up out of that same ol' bed every morning and go to that same ol' bathroom and look into that same ol' mirror at that same ol' face. Then we put on the same ol' clothes and eat them same ol' flakes and then get into that same ol' car and drive to the same ol' job and go through the same ol' routine every same ol' day! Life can become a real drag.

Maybe you're suffering from that "same ol', same ol' disease." You've lost your zest for life and your passion for people and ministry. Even the best Christians fall into spiritual slumps. Service after service, they just go through the motions. Whatever you do, don't quit. Ideally, we need to stay fresh; however, slumps are very real, and the only way to break out of a slump is to hang in there and keep swinging.

Frustrated by failure and discouraged by defeat, these slumping fishermen went back out to sea with Jesus in the boat. Jesus urged them to let down their nets for a catch.

"At Your word, I will let down the net," responded Pete. Miracles are contingent upon obedience to His Word. Wait for a word from God, and then obediently act! Many times, His Word will contradict our traditional thinking, philosophy, and game plan. Nevertheless, "Whatever He says to you, do it" (see Jn. 2:5)!

As soon as Pete and Andy obeyed, a miracle occurred. It happened suddenly. The net was now full—so full that it was breaking. The duo had to call for their partners Jim and John to come and help, and the catch was still so large that both boats began to sink. It was a net-breaking, boat-sinking catch! Never had these fishermen enjoyed so much success on this lake, or on any lake for that matter!

What is this saying to us? Whenever we push away from the shoreline of our own futility and failure with Christ in control, miracles will surely happen. When we stop toiling and begin trusting, positive results will eventually follow. When we let down our nets in obedience to a divine directive, everything will become too small—nets, boats, pews, classrooms, parking lots, and church sanctuaries. There will not be room enough to receive the blessing (see Mal. 3:10).

Are your nets still empty? Don't lose heart, and don't quit, my friend. You're in for the catch of a lifetime.

17

Crowd Support

One of the highest human duties is the duty of encouragement (William Barclay).

During the Boston Marathon, as I finally started up Heartbreak Hill, I was overcome with weariness and dizziness. Suddenly it occurred to me that the crowds were larger and the cheering more intense there than at any other point on the course.

The Boston Marathon had begun in the small New England town of Hopkinton, Massachusetts. As the gun sounded, starting the race, there had been a thunderous ovation from several hundred well-wishers. In fact, all along the course there had been people (a crowd estimated at over one million lined the marathon route) shouting encouragement to the runners.

But Heartbreak Hill was different. These spectators knew that this was the most difficult part of the course. It would be the runner's greatest test. This was the point where many competitors would drop out of the race. These people were there, committed to getting runners over that hill. "Keep going!" they shouted. "Don't quit! Hang tough! You're looking good!"

I really needed this encouragement. Suddenly fresh strength surged through my body. As the massive crowds cheered and chanted, my legs felt light; my vision cleared. I was so moved with elation and encouragement that chills ran through my body and tears came to my eyes. I got up on my toes and began to push, feeling stronger with every stride. When I crested Heartbreak Hill—even with more than five miles to go—I knew that I had conquered the Boston Marathon.

Halfway up Heartbreak Hill, while the crowd cheered and chanted words of encouragement, the Spirit of the Lord opened my spiritual eyes and revealed to me one of the greatest biblical truths: At the most difficult points of the Christian race, the crowds are also the largest and loudest. At your point of greatest hurt, you are surrounded by an innumerable company of spectators. We are surrounded by "a great cloud of witnesses" (Heb. 12:1 NIV). In one accord, this "cloud of witnesses" (or crowd of spectators)—led by the great cheerleader Jesus Christ—is chanting and cheering, "Don't quit! Hang tough! You can make it! Don't give up now! You're almost there!"

Who are these spectators? First of all, there's a heavenly host of angels. These are referred to as "ministering spirits" (Heb. 1:14). They are real, and they are here to minister strength and encouragement as you struggle up your personal Heartbreak Hill.

As Elisha the prophet lodged in the city of Dothan, his frightened servant warned him of the Syrian army that had already surrounded the city. The king of Syria had ordered his most elite infantry to capture Elisha. "What shall we do?" questioned the servant.

"Don't worry!" responded Elisha. "Because there are more with us than with them" (see 2 Kings 6:16). Elisha then prayed for the spiritual eyes of his servant to be opened. When the Lord opened his eyes, the servant could see multitudes of angelic beings covering the mountains around Dothan. Talk about crowd support!

If you're ready to hit the wall, struggling up your personal Heartbreak Hill, or just going through some painful ordeal, I invite you to open your spiritual eyes and understand that you are not alone. In the heavenlies, there stands a great multitude, and they are committed to seeing you through!

Second, in this arena of agony, we are surrounded by a great multitude of glorified saints who have already crossed the finish line. Having finished their race, they now sit in the arena in order to cheer us on. They're shouting, "Keep going! Hang tough! Don't quit! Press on! Don't lose heart! Don't grow weary! You can make it! We won, and you can win too!" Open your spiritual ears and listen for just a moment to all the encouragement being offered.

Noah is there. He's shouting, "Don't lose heart! If I built the ark and endured the flood, surely you can make it!"

Abraham is there. He's yelling, "Don't stagger at the promise of God! If I waited 25 years from promise to fulfillment, surely you can wait and reap the eventual benefit!"

Joseph is there. Listen to his words: "Press on, child of God! If I endured a pit, the advances of Potiphar's wife, and a prison term spanning over 13 painful years, surely you can hold on!"

Moses is there. He's saying, "Don't quit! If I endured 40 years in a desert before God's visitation, surely you can endure your dry places!"

Joshua is there: "Don't stop now! You've come too far to turn back. If I persevered 7 days and 13 tedious laps around Jericho, surely you can hang in there until your walls come down!"

David is there: "You can make it! If I endured the spears and the painful opposition of Saul before reaching success, surely you can make it!"

Elijah is there: "Faint not, child of God! If I endured the drying brook, an offensive mob of false prophets and over three years of drought, surely you can persevere through this trial!"

Daniel is there: "Fear not! If God protected me in a den of ferocious lions, surely He will keep you!"

The three Hebrew children are there: "Hang tough and don't run from the heat! If we endured a Babylonian furnace seven times hotter than normal, surely you can endure the intense heat of your trial!"

The 120 people empowered with the Holy Spirit on the Day of Pentecost are there: "Don't stop praying! If we prevailed in prayer for ten days before the promised power and harvest came, surely you can prevail!"

Paul the apostle is there: "Stand firm in the faith! If I didn't give up after being scourged five times, beaten with rods three times, stoned, imprisoned, and shipwrecked three times, surely you don't have to give up!"

These and multitudes of other glorified cheerleaders, being led by that great cheerleader, Jesus Christ—who endured bitter opposition and persevered on Calvary's agonizing hill—continue to shout, "We have overcome, and you can overcome! We have finished, and you can finish! We won, and you can win! We made it, and you can make it!"

In addition to the angelic host and the glorified saints from ages past, God is always faithful to surround us with loving, caring, encouraging people. Somewhere nearby there is a supportive church that is filled with concerned Christians waiting to embrace and assist you as you face the trials of life. Open your spiritual eyes! Contrary to how you may feel, you are not alone! Those people are there. Trust God to lead you to that much-needed support group.

You are surrounded by a great crowd of encouraging spectators who are committed to seeing you through. You're running before the home crowd. The crowd is on your side, and you have your teammates' support.

Encouragement is an awesome, powerful force, with the ability to lift, soothe, comfort, and strengthen. It is like a breath of fresh air. No one can survive long without it.

Many times I've seen an encouraging and supportive home crowd propel a weak and ineffective team to an inspiring victory over a more powerful opponent. Through many races, I have felt the encouragement of supportive fans. Through many sermons, I have felt the encouragement of supportive parishioners. I know the inspirational thrust of a supportive wife and family. Oh, what a difference encouragement makes!

Discouragement can strip a life of joy and faith; encouragement restores joy and faith to a life. William Barclay, one of the world's greatest Bible commentators, once said,

"One of the highest of human duties is the duty of encouragement... It is easy to laugh at men's ideals; it is easy to pour cold water on their enthusiasm; it is easy to discourage others. The world is full of discouragers. We have a Christian duty to encourage one another. Many a time a word of praise or thanks or appreciation or cheer has kept a man on his feet. Blessed is the man who speaks such a word."[1]

Many on Heartbreak Hill will never make it apart from encouragement. Can you think of someone who is discouraged? A hurting single mom, a student away at college, a divorcee struggling with acceptance, or a young couple who can't seem to make ends meet? Perhaps you know of a friend with only three months to live or a minister laboring in obscurity who feels forgotten?

From your sideline position, shout a word of encouragement: "Go for it! Hang in there! You're looking good! You can make it! Don't give up!" Shout! Cheer! Put your hands

---

1. William Barclay, "The Letter to the Hebrews," *The Daily Study Bible* (Edinburgh: St. Andrews Press, 1955), 137-138.

together and applaud someone! Your encouraging support just may keep someone on his feet and on course who otherwise would have fallen and quit.

At times, we might not hear the cheers of the encouraging host or feel the hand of a supportive friend, but even then we must not quit. We must be like David, who when his home was burned, his family and possessions were plundered, and he received no encouragement from other members of the team, "encouraged himself in the Lord his God" (1 Sam. 30:6 KJV). Quoting the Word of God is the surest way to encourage yourself.

Judges chapter 20 relates a story of civil war within the nation of Israel. The tribe of Benjamin had engaged in a vile act of immorality. When the rest of the tribes heard the gory details of this crime, they united as one man against Benjamin. When the battle lines were formed and the fighting underway, Israel suffered a most bitter defeat. But according to Judges 20:22, "...the men of Israel, encouraged themselves and again formed the battle line at the place where they had put themselves in array on the first day."

I find it interesting that a dose of self-encouragement could fortify a defeated army and prompt them to return to the very place where they had previously met with defeat. Isn't it great to know that defeat does not have to be final! Losing one battle doesn't mean that you've lost the war. Read the text, and you will see that it took Israel three battles to secure victory. And the underlying motivation that caused these defeated soldiers to return to the battle front was encouragement—self-encouragement.

Maybe you've conceded the victory, considering the enemy too powerful. I challenge you to encourage yourself in the Lord, rise up from the ashes of defeat and fight again. Hurting friend, you can make it!

[Be] *confident of this, that He who began a good work in you will carry it on to completion..."* (Philippians 1:6 NIV).

God got you started; He's helped you get where you are; and you can be sure He will not quit on you. Don't quit on God because He isn't going to quit on you.

18

The Race

The race is not always to the swift, but to those who keep on running.

I

"Quit! Give up! You're beaten!"
    They shout at me and plead.
"There's just too much against you now.
    This time you can't succeed!"

And as I start to hang my head
    In front of failure's face,
My downward fall is broken by
    The memory of a race.

And hope refills my weakened will
    As I recall that scene;
For just the thought of that short race
    Rejuvenates my being.

II

A children's race—young boys, young men—
    How I remember well.
Excitement sure! But also fear;
    It wasn't hard to tell.

They all lined up so full of hope;
    Each thought to win that race,
Or tie for first, or if not that,
    At least take second place.

And fathers watched from off the side,
    Each cheering for his son.
And each boy hoped to show his dad
    That he would be the one.

The whistle blew and off they went!
    Young hearts and hopes afire.
To win and be the hero there
    Was each young boy's desire.

And one boy in particular
    Whose dad was in the crowd
Was running near the lead and thought:
    "My dad will be so proud!"

But as they sped down the field
    Across a shallow dip,
The little boy who thought to win
    Lost his step and slipped.

Trying hard to catch himself
    His hands flew out to brace,
And amid the laughter of the crowd
    He fell flat on his face.

So down he fell and with him hope
    —He couldn't win it now—
Embarrassed, sad, he only wished
    To disappear somehow.

But as he fell his dad stood up
    And showed his anxious face,
Which to the boy so clearly said,
    "Get up and win the race."

He quickly rose, no damage done.
    —Behind a bit, that's all—

And ran with all his mind and might
To make up for his fall.

So anxious to restore himself
—To catch up and to win—
His mind went faster than his legs:
He slipped and fell again!

He wished then he had quit before
with only one disgrace.
"I'm hopeless as a runner now;
I shouldn't try to race."

But in the laughing crowd he searched
And found his father's face;
That steady look which said again;
"Get up and win the race."

So up he jumped to try again
—Ten yards behind the last—
"If I'm to gain those yards," he thought
"I've got to move real fast."

Exerting everything he had
He regained eight or ten
But trying so hard to catch the lead
He slipped and fell again!

Defeat! He lay there silently
—A tear dropped from his eye—
"There's no sense running any more;
"Three strikes; I'm out! Why try?"

The will to rise had disappeared
All hope had fled away
So far behind, so error prone;
A failure all the way.

"I've lost, so what's the use," he thought.
"I'll live with my disgrace."
But then he thought about his dad
Who soon he'd have to face.

"Get up," an echo sounded low.
  "Get up and take your place;
You were not meant for failure here.
  Get up and win the race."

"With borrowed will get up," it said
  "You haven't lost at all.
For winning is no more than this:
  To rise each time you fall."

So up he rose to run once more,
  And with a new commit
He resolved that win or lose
  At least he wouldn't quit.

So far behind the others now,
  —The most he'd ever been—
Still he gave it all he had
  And ran as though to win.

Three times he's fallen, stumbling;
  Three times he rose again;
Too far behind to hope to win,
  He still ran to the end.

They cheered the winning runner
  As he crossed the line first place,
Head high, and proud, and happy;
  No falling, no disgrace.

But then the fallen youngster
  crossed the line last place,
The crowd gave him the greater cheer
  For finishing the race.

And even though he came in last
  With head bowed low, unproud,
You would have thought he'd won the race
  To listen to the crowd.

And to his dad he sadly said,
  "I didn't do so well."

"To me, you won," his father said.
  "You rose each time you fell."

III

And now when things seem dark and hard
  And difficult to face,
The memory of that little boy
  Helps me in my race.

For all my life is like that race,
  With ups and downs and all,
And all you have to do to win,
  Is rise each time you fall.

"Quit! Give up! You're beaten!"
  They still shout in my face.
But another voice within me says:
  "GET UP AND WIN THE RACE!"[1]

---

1. D.H. Groberg, "The Race" (Sandy, Utah, 1984). Used by permission.

19

Fire at the Finish

"Desire fire: we will do more for God as fools on fire than as intellectuals on ice."

—Robert G. Lee

In the early Greek games, marathon runners raced against each other for the coveted victory wreath. One thing was different in those original Olympic games: Each runner had to carry a lighted torch. The winner of the race was not necessarily the one "who finished first, but the one who finished first with his torch still lit." Each runner had to cautiously guard the flame every minute of every mile.

In the Christian arena, finishing first isn't the goal. Our primary goal must be to finish with the torch still lit and the fire of God's love and presence still burning in our hearts. Finishing isn't enough; we must finish on fire!

How do we stay on fire to the finish?

1. Make sure there is a flame.

Many who complain about being "burned-out" were never on fire to start with. How can you burn out if you've never been on fire? Today's Christians often have all the facts, but no flames—form, but no fire. Facts and formalism must give way to fervency and holy flame. The Laodicean church was judged for its lack of fire (see Rev. 3). Let us not think that we shall escape the judgment of God for our indifference and lukewarmness.

Fire has always been a symbol of the presence of God, and genuine spiritual fire must originate from above. Jewish tradition holds that the fire of the brazen altar was first kindled by the Lord: "And fire came out from before the Lord..." (Lev. 9:24). The Lord started the fire. He is the source of all genuine Pentecostal flame. Again, at the dedication of Solomon's Temple, "Fire came down from heaven..." (2 Chron. 7:1). Stop trying to work something up; instead, pursue the fire that comes down from above!

Jesus spoke of John the Baptist as a "burning and shining lamp" (Jn. 5:35). Charles Finney, the great American revivalist, prayed, "Lord, set me on fire that people will come and watch me burn." God desires to ignite each of us with holy flames so that we will also be burning lamps for Him. Romans 12:11 defines the believer's service in these words: "...Fervent [or hot and burning] in spirit, serving the Lord."

Inspect your heart and make sure there is a holy fire burning within it. Sparks of emotionalism and sensationalism will not suffice. Holy flames are needed!

2. Fan the flame.

Holy flames and spiritual gifts do not automatically remain strong and vital in our lives. For that reason, Paul insisted, "...I remind you to fan into flame the gift of God" (2 Tim. 1:6a NIV). The Amplified Bible reads, "...(rekindle the embers...fan the flame...and keep burning)...[the inner fire]...."

The inner flame has been neglected long enough. It is weak and flickering. For this reason Paul preached with great urgency, "Fan the flame!" Fan, feed, fuel. Do whatever is necessary to keep the fire alive. Personal responsibility is implied here: You fan the flame! Holy flames are fanned by prayer and fueled by the Word of God. Every day you neglect prayer and

Bible study, the fire diminishes. If the inner fire dies, it's nobody's fault but your own.

3. Guard the flame.

On two occasions, Paul instructed Timothy to guard the flame (1 Tim. 6:20; 2 Tim. 1:14 NIV). We are to guard the inner flame of the Holy Spirit as a runner guards the flame of his torch.

As we run this race we must concentrate not just on running or keeping pace, but on guarding our flame. Fierce winds of adversity and torrential rains of opposition will blow and put out our flame if we don't guard it! We guard our family, the yard, the car, even the house, but when it comes to the inner flame, we are often sorely negligent.

Guard against anything and everything that threatens to extinguish your inner flame. Guard against the lust of the eye, the lust of the flesh, and the pride of life (see 1 Jn. 2:16). Guard against wordliness and selfishness. Guard against prejudice and covetousness, bitterness and unforgiveness. Guard your heart and its burning passion for God! Guard it with the sword of the Spirit!

As you guard your heart's fire, you guard against quitting. That inner flame is vital to your progress. When the fire dies, quitting becomes inevitable. The Old Testament priests were commanded as follows: "And the fire on the altar shall be kept burning on it; it shall not be put out...A fire shall always be burning on the altar; it shall never go out" (Lev. 6:12-13). The Lord started the fire, but it was the job of the priest to maintain and preserve that holy flame. As New Testament believer-priests, we are under the same obligation to keep the holy fire of God alive.

If necessary, slow your pace lest worldly winds or religious rains extinguish your torch. Each of us must resolve to slow down. This race is not to the swift! We must learn to gracefully say "No" to well-meaning people and even to legitimate activity that would rob our time and sap our energies.

Learn to aggressively resist the temptation to chase after more pleasures, more hobbies, and more social entanglements. Be willing to block out every intrusion with the tenacity of a pro-football tackle. Whatever you do, preserve that inner flame and keep your heart hot for God. You must stay on fire to the finish line. You must finish strong. Finish in a blaze of holy passion!

Carry the torch and guard the flame as you run this race! Remember, the winners of this race are those who finish on fire.

Finish the Race

What shall it profit a man if he has a triumphant beginning but a tragic ending? It's not how you start but how you finish that counts!

A little-known Tanzanian runner finished dead last in the 1968 Olympic Games in Mexico City. Along the way he sustained an injury that set him back. Rather than drop out of the race, however, he struggled on and eventually crossed the finish line long after the other runners had finished.

A reporter approached him and asked, "Why did you bother to finish? It was obvious you couldn't win."

"My country didn't send me 7,000 miles to start the race, but to finish the race!" responded the Tanzanian.

Many of you have sustained injuries along the course. You've been hurt, offended, criticized, or falsely accused. "Why bother?" you question. "Why go on? Why even try? It's obvious I can't achieve or succeed."

I remind you, God hasn't called you to start the race but to finish it—whatever the cost. Hang tough and go the distance, even if you have to hobble or crawl.

My driving passion in life is to finish the race and finish it well. How I long to hear the words, "Well done, thou good and faithful servant...!" A runner who cannot finish cannot win. Teams that cannot finish end up on the losing end. We must learn how to finish!

The Bible portrays some 400 leaders. Surprisingly, only about 80 of them finished well. Some of the non-finishers might surprise you: For example, what about Samson, Saul, and Solomon? None of these men finished the race triumphantly.

Samson was a Nazarite unto God from his mother's womb. Set apart from other men, he was also marvelously empowered and moved upon by the Holy Spirit. With his bare hands, he tore a lion apart. With the jawbone of an ass, he single-handedly slew 1,000 Philistines. Samson was called of God to deliver Israel from the domination of the Philistines. But rather than overcoming the enemy, he was overcome. Despite his marvelous beginning, Samson died tragically.

Saul was Israel's first king, an anointed leader. Empowered by the Holy Spirit, he united a people, founded a kingdom, organized an army, and defeated many enemies. But the last years of his life were dark and ugly. In the end, Saul was consumed by jealousy, throwing his spears, killing priests, consulting with witches, and being controlled by evil spirits. Finally, he committed suicide. Saul's triumphant start was overshadowed by his tragic end.

Solomon was the wisest man who ever lived, endowed with insight from God. He authored 3,000 proverbs and over 1,000 songs. He even built the majestic Temple—something that his father David was not chosen to do. But Solomon's downfall can be traced to his unbridled passion for foreign women. Ultimately, he had 700 wives and 300 concubines, none of which worshiped God. It is recorded that, "...[Solomon's] wives turned his heart after other gods" (1 Kings 11:4a).

Oh, how the mighty have fallen!

Both Karl Marx and Joseph Stalin began as seminary students. Adolph Hitler once studied for the priesthood. It doesn't matter how marvelous a beginning you might have had, if you're not able to finish! People will not remember you for how you started the race—only by how you came across the finish line.

The ultimate joy in living, as in running, is to finish, and finish well. Paul the apostle possessed a driving passion to finish. He declared in Second Timothy 4:7, "I have fought the good fight, I have finished the race, I have kept the faith."

We must allow that same driving passion to grip our hearts as we endeavor to serve the Lord. We haven't been called to merely start but to go the distance. The call is to *finish*. Jesus said, "...My food is to do the will of Him who sent Me, and to finish His work" (Jn. 4:34). In the Garden of Gethsemene He prayed, "I have finished the work which You have given Me to do" (Jn. 17:4b). Then from Calvary's cross, He concluded, "It is finished!" (Jn. 19:30)

It is so easy to start, but it is so very difficult to finish. I've run in over 500 races—from the quarter mile to the marathon—and only on a few occasions did finishing seem easy. Finishing is tough!

What does it take to finish? Finishing requires three vital ingredients:

1. Durability

Durability is the ability to endure or last without significant deterioration. Toughness. The ability to withstand pressure without breaking. The smart consumer shops for durable products, whether its tools that don't break during use or clothes that wear well and long.

Paul the apostle was durable. He said, "But none of these things move me; nor do I count my life dear to myself, so that I may finish my race with joy" (Acts 20:24a). What things was Paul referring to? Five scourgings of 39 lashes each, three beatings with rods, stonings, imprisonment, and three shipwrecks (just to name a few). (See Second Corinthians 11:24-28.) None of these things could knock Paul off his spiritual feet. Talk about stability and durability!

Those who love their lives almost always quit in the tough places. That's why Paul said, "Nor do I count my life dear unto myself, so that I may finish my race." The only way to victoriously endure and successfully finish is to continually deny yourself.

When Paul said, "I have fought the good fight" (2 Tim. 4:7), he meant it. He stayed in the ring, round after difficult round. He kept jabbing, punching, fighting, refusing to go down. Nothing could stop Paul from fulfilling the heavenly vision and finishing the work. Hell threw everything imaginable at him, but he withstood it all—unmoved! What would it take to stop this blazing missionary? Apparently more than hell could muster up.

Today's Christian is so easily moved. We are so easily intimidated, so easily offended, so easily hurt. Have you noticed how the slightest thing affects us? Many quit the very moment they are offended or criticized. At the first sign of problems or pressure, we stop trying. But Paul commanded, "...Be steadfast, immovable..." (1 Cor. 15:58). Stand tall in the arena of faith, absorb the jabs, and refuse to quit.

Even ministers lack durability. In certain denominations, the average pastor lasts only one and a half years per church. The average tenure varies among denominations, but the highest average is only three years. Worse, the average pastor lasts less than 14 years in the ministry!

An interesting study of Yale College graduates from 1702 to 1775 revealed that 79 percent of those graduates who became ministers served one congregation all their lives. Talk about durability! Back then, "transient pastors" were nearly non-existent. Ministering in the twenty-first century is not for wimps, but warriors. We must become durable disciples!

Durability is the ability to absorb jabs. Paul insisted that every Christian, "Put on the whole armor of God, that you may be able to stand against the [deceitful jabs] of the devil. ...take up the whole armor of God, that you may be able to withstand in the evil day, and having done all, to stand" (Eph. 6:11,13). Remember, durability is the ability to withstand pressure and stress without breaking. The armor of God is crucial if we're going to withstand the affliction and adversity of this evil day without breaking or quitting!

To each of the seven churches in Asia, Jesus gave a promise, and each promise was based on one condition: "Overcome!" To overcome means to prevail until you finish.

There is far too much quitting going on today. Something needs to be said about hanging tough, riding out storms, absorbing jabs, and prevailing until one finishes. "Well, I tried," you might say. Big deal! Trying isn't good enough. There are no rewards for trying, only finishing, and those who quit are disqualified. Quitters forfeit their rewards.

Hebrews 3:14 reminds us, "For we have become partakers of Christ if we hold the beginning of our confidence steadfast to the end." We must hold fast until the end!

Paul questions, "Who shall separate us from the love of Christ? Shall trouble or hardship or persecution or famine or nakedness or danger or sword?" (Rom. 8:35 NIV) Emphatically, he shouts,

> *No, in all these things we are more than conquerors through Him who loved us. For I am convinced that neither...the present nor the future, nor any powers, neither height nor depth, nor anything else in all creation, will be able to separate us from the love of God that is in Christ Jesus our Lord* (Romans 8:37-39 NIV).

As did the first-century Church, the end-time Church must be able to stand tall in the evangelistic ring and absorb some jabs without quitting. Much gets started in the arena of evangelism that never gets finished. We must see every effort through to completion! It's not enough to merely fight, we must finish! And that requires durability.

2. Direction

Before we can accomplish anything, we need clear direction. Life without direction is futile. Unfortunately, many people today are in the wrong lane, driving down the wrong road, following the wrong map, and heading in the wrong direction without the foggiest idea of what life is about.

Some years ago, in Malaysia, a seven-mile cross-country race was conducted. Two hours after the race had begun (which was adequate time for even the slowest runners to cover the course), no runners had crossed the finish line. Fearing that something must have gone wrong, the race officials set out in automobiles to find the runners.

All the runners were found about six miles away. All were sprinting in the wrong direction. Many of the runners had, in fact, already covered a distance of over ten miles. As one official explained, "The mix-up apparently occurred when the lead runner took a wrong turn at the fifth checkpoint, and everyone followed him."

Beware of your direction—who you're following and where they're taking you! Many so-called role models, even supposed men of God, have made wrong turns. The worst mistake you could make in life would be to run after another person as fast as you can without ever asking where you're going. Sometimes we're so concerned about getting somewhere that we lose sight of our destination. Please stop long enough to find out where your leaders are taking you!

We're in a real race, and this race has a judge, a map, and a finish line. God is the judge who has carefully laid out the course. The Bible is the map divinely designed to keep us on the course and successfully bring us to the finish line.

The Bible commands us to "...walk circumspectly, not as fools but as wise" (Eph. 5:15). Essentially, the command is this: Live your life with purpose and direction and know where you are going. In an age of confusion and unprecedented deception, we need sound, biblical, Holy Ghost direction.

3. Determination

Successful fighting and finishing requires determination. Determination is a mental attitude that never says quit. It also never really kicks in until you make a firm decision or until you dedicate yourself to a particular cause.

God has called us to go the distance: Determination is the factor that drives a person toward success and victory. Determined people are hard to stop! We will only reap a harvest if we do not give up (see Gal. 6:9 NIV).

There was once a preacher who loved to hunt. He bought two bird dogs—setters—and put them in his backyard. One morning, a mean vicious-looking bulldog came down the alley. This dog meant business. The preacher's first impulse was to put the setters in the basement for fear they might tear up the bulldog. His second impulse? Well, maybe he would just let his setters teach the bulldog a lesson.

When the bulldog crawled under the fence and into the yard, those two bird dogs attacked. Around and around the dogs went for several minutes. When the bulldog had had enough, he limped helplessly away, squirmed under the fence, and withdrew down the alley. There he laid for the remainder of the day, licking his sores and nursing his wounds. The preacher thought that would be the end of it.

But the very next day, at the same time, down the alley that bulldog came again—under the fence and into the backyard. Round Two began. After the two setters bloodied him once more, the bulldog again retreated. Under the fence and back down the alley he went, licking his sores and nursing his wounds. Surely, this time the lesson had been learned.

But on the third day, at the same time, down the alley came that bulldog—under the fence and into the yard. And again, the setters eventually drove him off, bruised and bleeding.

About this time the preacher had to leave town for several days on business. When he finally returned home, he curiously asked his wife about the bulldog.

She smiled wryly. "Honey, you won't believe this, but every day, at the same time, down the alley came that bulldog, under the fence and into our yard. Day after day, the setters pounced on him and bloodied him. But today, when our setters saw the bulldog coming back, they began to whine and cry. Finally, they ran down into the basement. They don't want anything to do with that bulldog. That bulldog is now the master of our backyard!"

Although quitters are never winners, winners are never quitters. The bulldog became a winner simply because he refused to quit. It's not the dog in the fight that counts, but the fight in the dog. Each of us needs to exercise the triumphant tenacity of this bulldog.

Do you feel beaten down? Battered and bruised? Overcome with failure? Maybe you've been hurt or offended—don't let that stop you. You may be knocked down, but you haven't been knocked out. Get up and continue on! Determined people don't quit. In fact, the determined person doesn't have the word *quit* in his vocabulary.

When Paul the apostle declared, "I have kept the faith" (2 Tim. 4:7), he was literally saying, "I have held on! I have determined not to let go!" Are you holding on to the ropes? The baton? The torch?

Jesus said, "But hold fast [or hold firmly] what you have till I come" (Rev. 2:25). Hold tightly to the biblical truths and values that you have. Refuse to let go. Maybe you've come to the end of your rope; tie a knot and hold on. Don't let go! And as you hold on, hang tough!

It is impossible to achieve, succeed, finish, or win without determination. Could lack of revival and effective evangelism be the result of our lack of determination? Our mentality is so short-term. We go to a seminar, get an idea, bring it home, try it for a few short weeks. If it doesn't work, we give up and terminate the effort.

It's time to wake up! The work of evangelism requires persistence and determination. Jesus said, "...No one, having put his hand to the plow, and looking back, is fit for the kingdom of God" (Lk. 9:62). The success of the early Church was not the result of ideal circumstances or talented people. It was, however, the result of determined men and women who had a passion for evangelism and who would not quit in the face of criticism, opposition, and persecution. We also must act with determination if we are to be effective for God.

Is the race easy? Of course not! Do we ever get discouraged? Every one of us! Are we ever tempted to quit? Absolutely! But we can't quit because we have been called to finish.

Paul was careful to make every stride and every punch count: "Therefore I do not run like a man running aimlessly; I do not fight like a man beating the air" (1 Cor. 9:26 NIV). "I have fought the good fight," he declared, "I have finished the race" (see 2 Tim. 4:7).

As Paul wrote these words, he was waiting in Nero's dungeon. Soon the executioner would come and lead him to the chopping block. He then declared, "Now there is in store for me the crown of righteousness, which the Lord, the righteous Judge, will award to me on that day..." (2 Tim. 4:8 NIV). Paul never lost sight of the prize that is reserved at the finish line. In fact, he challenged us to run in such a way that we might also obtain it (see 1 Cor. 9:24). Our inheritance is incorruptible—one that will never fade or tarnish—and it's reserved for us in Heaven (see 1 Pet. 1:4). If our inheritance were here, there would be no need for hope. The best is yet to come!

In the Roman athletic games, a laurel wreath was given to the winners. This wreath was a symbol of victory, the most coveted prize in ancient Rome. "They compete for a perishable crown," Paul was careful to distinguish, "but we for an imperishable crown" (see 1 Cor. 9:25).

Blessed is the man who perseveres under trial, because when he has stood the test, he will receive the crown of life that God has promised to those who love Him (James 1:12 NIV).

Do not become weary in your race, studies, responsibilities, marriage, or ministry. Stay on the course that God has marked out for you. Hold on! Hang tough! The end will be worth it, so don't quit! Go the distance! Press on, run hard, run to finish! Run to win!

There is no greater joy than the joy of finishing. Ecstasy breaks out at the finish line. Don't miss the thrill and the tribute of, "Well done, good and faithful servant...Enter into the joy of your Lord" (see Mt. 25:21).

Don't Quit

When things go wrong as they sometimes will,
When the road you're trudging seems all uphill,
When the funds are low and the debts are high,
And you want to smile, but have to sigh,
When care is pressing you down a bit,
Rest if you must, but don't you quit!

Life is queer with its twists and turns,
As everyone of us sometimes learns;
And many a fellow turns about,
When he might have won had he stuck it out.
Don't give up though the race seems slow...
You may succeed with another blow.

Often the goal is nearer than
It seems to a faint and faltering man;
Often the struggler has given up,
When he might have captured the Victor's Cup;
And he learned too late when the night came down,
How close he was to the winning crown.

Success is failure turned inside out,
The silver tint of the clouds of doubt,
And you never can tell how close you are,
It may be near when it seems so far;
So stick to the fight when you're hardest hit,
It's when things seem worst that you mustn't quit.[1]

---

1. Author unknown.

Conclusion

They're in the final turn. The runners suddenly burst into sprinter's speed. This is the home stretch; they can see the finish line. Each runner is focused and determined, running with greater intensity and desire.

The pace is hard and fast. Each competitor gives his last ounce of enduring strength, striving hard to avoid defeat.

Within seconds, they reach the finish line. Each athlete stretches, lunges forward, determined to win the race.

I've been a part of this scenario countless times over the years. No part of a race, regardless of its length, is any more strategic than the last one or two hundred meters. This is the home stretch—the race within the race. Most often, this final stretch determines the winner.

Every successful race strategy involves a vicious kick down the final stretch. A runner who relaxes down the stretch is a sure loser. Stretch time is crunch time: The competitive runner knows that it's now or never, do or die. He must perform!

The closer a runner gets to the finish line the faster he runs, and the more focused he becomes. As he enters the stretch, he pulls out all the stops, picks up the pace, and drives hard. He literally "turns it on."

Likewise, I think it is safe to assume that we're in the home stretch. We are living in the last minutes, maybe the last seconds, of the last days. Our finish line is within sight. The end is near—nearer than we have imagined.

It would be unthinkable for an accomplished runner, with his sights on winning, to relax, slow the pace, or quit while running down the home stretch. Likewise, for a believer to relax his efforts, slow the pace, or quit while in the final stretch would be unforgivable.

Friend, pull out the stops! Give the stretch run your very best shot! Respond to the challenge with great courage and fearless intensity: "Run in such a way that you may obtain!" (see 1 Cor. 9:24). The end may be nearer than you think.

Epilogue:
Pointers on Perseverance

- Realize that the temptation to quit is real. Everyone is tempted to quit at some point.

- Determine ahead of time that you won't quit. "...Be steadfast, immovable, always abounding in the work of the Lord..." (1 Cor. 15:58).

- Guard against quitting by surrounding yourself with encouragement.

- Be prepared with Scripture that will encourage and motivate you to press on.

- Have someone—a pastor, teacher, or Christian friend—who can give you encouragement.

- Falling down doesn't mean you are a failure—staying down does.

- It's better to fail than to quit.

- Never forget who called you. God has called you to finish. He wants you to go the distance and not quit.

- Quitters are never winners. Winners are never quitters.

- Rest if you must, but don't quit!

Other
Destiny Image titles
you will enjoy reading

DON'T DIE IN THE WINTER...
by Dr. Millicent Thompson.
Why do we go through hard times? Why must we suffer pain? In *Don't Die in the Winter...* Dr. Thompson explains the spiritual seasons and cycles that people experience. A spiritual winter is simply a season that tests our growth. We need to endure our winters, for in the plan of God, spring always follows winter!
Paperback Book, 168p. ISBN 1-56043-558-5 Retail $8.99

I STOOD IN THE FLAMES
by Dr. Wanda A. Davis-Turner.
If you have ever come to a point of depression, fear, or defeat, then you need this book! With honesty, truth, and clarity, Dr. Davis-Turner shares her hard-won principles for victory in the midst of the fire. You can turn satan's attack into a platform of strength and laughter!
Paperback Book, 154p. ISBN 1-56043-275-6 Retail $8.99

THE POWER OF BROKENNESS
by Don Nori.
Accepting Brokenness is a must for becoming a true vessel of the Lord, and is a stepping-stone to revival in our hearts, our homes, and our churches. Brokenness alone brings us to the wonderful revelation of how deep and great our Lord's mercy really is. Join this companion who leads us through the darkest of nights. Discover the *Power of Brokenness*.
Paperback Book, 168p. ISBN 1-56043-178-4 Retail $9.99

GET OFF YOUR OWN BACK
by Dr. Freda V. Crews.
We feel what we feel and do what we do because *we believe what we believe*! Unfortunately, many of our beliefs are based on *myths* rooted in falsehoods. Thus we weave webs that entangle us in self-destructive behavior patterns. Only the truth can untangle these webs. This life-changing book arms you with the reality of God's Word and will destroy the myths that rob you of your personhood.
Paperback Book, 168p. ISBN 1-56043-292-6 (6" X 9") Retail $9.99

Available at your local Christian bookstore.

Internet: http://www.reapernet.com

Prices subject to change without notice.